SEVEN LIES

ALMOST EVERY TEEN BELIEVES

BY JOEL PENTON

SEVEN LIES ALMOST EVERY TEEN BELIEVES
By Joel Penton

Published by Madison Press
Printed by Lightning Source

Edited by Shannah Hogue

Cover Design by Zoi Samara and Daron Short
Page Design and Layout by Velin Saramov

Penton, Joel, 2011
[Seven Lies Almost Every Teen Believes]
Young Adults/Religion/General

ISBN 978-0-615-51618-9

Manufactured in the United States of America

Before you begin reading, I thought you should know that I made some short videos to go along with this book. I've posted them, as well as some other digital awesomeness online for free. When you get a chance, check it out at SEVENLIESONLINE.COM

Enjoy the book!

-Joel

PS - You should also know that no human beings were harmed while making the front cover of this book. (The guy on the front is just a freshman so he doesn't count.)

CONTENTS

For My Best Friend

WHAT'S THIS BOOK ABOUT?

You are being lied to.

That's right. You heard me. Right this very minute, you are being lied to. Everywhere you go, everywhere you look, you're getting played.

I know...you think you've heard this all before. You can see through all the crap out there trying to get your attention. You're too smart to get taken in.

Well...I say that's wishful thinking. I say you're cocky. I say you've been blinded. Even with all your defenses up...you've been sucked in. Someone has you captive, blindfolded so you can't see what's really going on.

You don't believe me? Of course you don't. Why would you, right? You don't even know who I am.

Someone has you captive, blindfolded so you can't see what's really going on.

My name is Joel. I used to play football for The Ohio State Buckeyes. Now I travel the country, speaking in schools. Yep...hitting people paid my way through college, and now I get paid to yell at people. I'm not like a big deal or anything. Seriously. I'm just a normal guy from a small town who did pretty well at football. That's about it.

But...I'm also one of the few people out there who will tell you how things really are. Not just what I think you want to hear. Not just what other people think you should hear. I'm going to lay it all out so you can see things for yourself...maybe for the very first time.

Why?

Because you need to know. It's not about making you like me or winning some "Good Guy of the Year" award. I'm telling you this because you need to know.

So...are you willing to hear me out? Are you willing to take a second look at the lies you've been fed and see what's really going on?

Good...then let's get started.

THE LIES

Look around you. Right now. Right where you are.

What do you see?

Billboards, magazines, books. Television and movies. Music, art and YouTube. IM, Twitter, Facebook and iPhone apps.

And what do they all have in common?

Messages. Some of them are true...some of them are lies. But all of them are trying to persuade you to listen to them, to buy into what they are saying.

And it gets worse.

Think about the people around you. Friends, teachers, coaches, pastors, politicians, your parents — and every other voice in your life—just might be lying to you. Not all of them. Not every time. Maybe not even on purpose. But the people around you, the ones you trust the most...they just might be lying to you.

But the worst part of all?

You've been listening to it for so long, getting it from so many places and from so many people, that you don't even realize that there's a problem. The lies sound normal to you. The lies sound like truth. After all, if everyone is saying the same thing... it's probably right.

Right?

Maybe. Or maybe not. That's why you need to start paying attention...start wondering...start asking some tough questions, some really tough questions.

About what? Simple...about everything.

Everything from the little stuff like what you should eat, drive and wear. All the way to the big stuff like life and death and God and Jesus...

"Oh great, he mentioned Jesus. Here comes the corny 'Christian' talk."

Well, okay...you caught me. I'm a Christian. And a lot of what I'm going to say has to do with Christianity. But here's the thing...

I know that there are all types of people reading this book.

Some of you are reading this book, thinking, *"Joel, I'm already a Christian. I know all of that stuff. I've got it covered."* And others are thinking, *"Man, I've already heard all that stuff. I don't buy it, and nothing you have to say is going to change my mind."*

Guess what? I think you're both wrong.

I think the stuff that the first group says they *"know"* and the second group says they've *"heard"* is probably a bunch of lies.

See, what a lot of "religious" people have bought into is fake. They sit back comfortably, thinking they've got the "spiritual" stuff covered. But they have no clue what it is they say they've ACCEPTED.

I went to school because I had to. I played sports because I loved to. And I went to church because I was supposed to.

And what most people have rejected is the same fake "religious" stuff. It sounds irrelevant, irrational, and worthless, so they think they can do without it. But they have no clue what it is they say they've REJECTED.

Both groups have been blinded by lies.

And what we need is the truth. You need it. I need it. Of course...we just have to figure out what the truth is, right? Well, that's what this book is about.

See, I used to believe the lies, too. For a long time, I was a normal kid in a normal small town in Ohio who did all the normal things. I went to school because I had to. I played sports because I loved to. And I went to church because I was supposed to.

But I believed the lies. And it wasn't until high school that things changed.

So, I want to tell you my story. I want to give it to you straight. I want to challenge you, for the next seven chapters, just to hear me out.

My challenge for you is simple: consider the possibility that what you believe is true just might be a lie. Be willing to take off your blindfold, perhaps for the first time. And be open to the reality that the truth can change your life, just like it changed mine.

Of course, you don't have to just take my word for it or blindly trust what I have to I say. I'm going to show you my reasons for what I believe.

I hope you're ready...because here comes Lie #1.

MAKING IT PERSONAL

1. Do you feel like you are constantly being bombarded with messages? What are some of the main sources of these messages?

___

___

___

2. Think of your favorite TV commercial, TV show, or movie. What messages is it sending? Are those messages good or bad?

___

___

___

3. Are you willing to take the challenge to see if you've been sucked into believing the lies?

___

___

___

LIE #1:

"THE BIG STUFF CAN WAIT."

A Lesson From A Lawn Mower

In sixth grade, I started my own business.

My first task was making business cards. I designed them on my computer, printed them on flimsy neon green paper, and cut them to size with a pair of scissors. The "cards" clearly stated my name, address, and phone number. But my favorite part was the name I'd invented for my new company: "Pro-Mow."

That's right, I mowed lawns.

Of course, I now realize that my "business" was a joke. And that those business cards looked ridiculous. But back then, I thought they were awesome. I thought my business was awesome.

And in some ways, I was right.

See, when I was even younger, my very first job was delivering newspapers. And if you know anything at all about paper routes, you know they aren't fun. Actually, they can be pretty horrible.

Every day I took a stack of papers and spent hours folding and rubber-banding them. If it was raining, they also had to be bagged. Then, I started delivering. Most days, that went fine. But if it was really hot, or really cold, or windy, or rainy, or snowy, or whatever, it could get pretty uncomfortable.

Then I had to collect money from my customers. That was the worst part of all. Usually people weren't home the first time I tried. Sometimes people just wouldn't pay. Apparently, a fourth-grader on a bike isn't very intimidating.

I think I made about a dollar an hour working that paper route.

I know...sad story...boo hoo for me.

So when my next-door neighbor, Mitch, gave up mowing lawns to get a real job, I jumped at the chance to take them over. Of course, it was just two lawns in our neighborhood. But I didn't know that was lame. To me, it was the best job ever. I thought, "Wow, only a couple lawns a week, and I can make the same amount of money as my paper route?"

Easy decision. I was sold.

And then my fancy "Pro-Mow" business cards got me a few other lawns in the neighborhood, and I started making decent money. Sweet!

So, after that, my routine each summer day was pretty simple: wake up, work out, mow lawns, hang out. It was an excellent way to spend the summer. And, I was eventually able to save enough money to buy my first car.

But...not everything about that job was awesome. Most days I would procrastinate for a long time before making the tough decision to go out and mow.

"Why was it so tough, Joel? You already said you were making more money in less time than working the paper route."

Well, to be honest, I was kind of lazy. But more than that, mowing was tough for a different reason. Sometimes I avoided mowing those lawns so I wouldn't have to be alone...with my thoughts.

As a student-athlete in middle school and high school, my life was busy. Most of the time, my mind was occupied with TV, friends, music, football and family. But, when I mowed lawns, there weren't any distractions. I tried to listen to music, but my mower was so loud that I couldn't hear it. The constant sound of the engine drowned everything out...except my thoughts.

My mind always drifted to the big questions like, *"Why am I here on this earth? What is the meaning of life? Is there a God? What's going to happen when I die?"* And those questions made me uncomfortable. I didn't like not knowing the answers.

So I tried to think about other stuff. I thought about girls and sports and...more girls, but soon, my mind was back to those questions.

"Is this life all there is? What if I die..like soon?" Aaaahhhh!! I couldn't stop the thoughts. No matter how hard I tried, they just kept coming up.

And even though I figured that other people had the same thoughts when they were alone, no one seemed to talk about them much. Sometimes they got mentioned at church, but to me, all that church stuff seemed...unrealistic. Plastic. Fake.[1]

All that church stuff seemed... unrealistic. Plastic. Fake.

I didn't want canned answers. I wanted real answers. But no one seemed to have them, and no one seemed to care enough to find them or talk about them.

Eventually I decided, *"There's no point in trying*

to figure it out now. I'll just try not to think about it. The BIG Stuff can wait."

What a lie.

AN EVERYDAY LIE

We have a huge problem.

"What huge problem? Preventing nuclear holocaust? Establishing peace in the Middle East? Finding the exact number of times I can hit snooze while still making it out the door on time?"

No, it's an even bigger problem. It's...Life.

Your life. My life. The realities of Life. And most of all — DEALING with those realities.

Seriously, answering life's big questions can seem like too much at times. Too intimidating. Too overwhelming.

So what do most of us do? Nothing.

I think a lot of people are just like me sitting on that lawn mower. I had big questions. But I didn't really deal with them. I kept hoping they would just go away.

I bought into Lie #1.

Don't get me wrong. Lie #1 does have a very appealing ring to it. "Sure, life is complicated," it says, "but don't feel like you need to figure it out right now. You've got too much going on. The BIG Stuff can wait."

Unfortunately, it's just not true. The BIG Stuff absolutely can't wait.

THE BIG STUFF

So...what exactly are we talking about here? What is this "BIG Stuff" we're supposed to be so concerned about?

I'm so glad you asked.

The BIG Stuff is actually pretty easy to sum up. It really comes down to three basic things.

LIFE. DEATH. GOD.

Of course, we can break them down a bit further with more specific questions.

LIFE: Who am I? Why am I here?
DEATH: What happens when I die?
GOD: Does God exist? What is he like?

But pretty much...that's it. The big picture. The bigger-than-life questions that people everywhere need answers to.

"Like who?"

Like your friends and neighbors. The lunch lady. Hollywood superstars. Farmers in Poland. Chinese grandmothers. And everyone in between.

These are the questions that every single human in history has had to answer. These are the questions that YOU have to answer.

Unfortunately, it can feel like we're trapped inside a hotel without windows.

"Um...what?"

I know that sounds weird, but think about it.

Imagine you wake up one day to find yourself in a standard-looking hotel room. You have no idea how you got there. As you wander around the hotel, you notice that it's not just any

It's kind of like we are all trapped in a hotel without windows.

normal hotel. It's actually really weird. The building has no windows, and the only exit, the front door, is locked. You can't see who or what, if anything, is outside. As you meet the other guests, you quickly learn that they, just like you, each appeared in the hotel one day and have no idea why they are there. Weirder still, guests occasionally disappear at random. You might be talking to someone when, all of a sudden, they just vanish into thin air.

Okay, so that sounds like a cheesy sci-fi movie, right? But go with me for a minute.

What if you found yourself in that exact situation? What would you do? I know what I would do. I'd be trying to figure out what was going on.

But the thing is...we ARE in that hotel. That's the life we all live.

One day we appear (are born) into this big world, but we have no idea why we are here. We see people around us disappearing (dying) all the time, but we don't know what happens to them when they leave this place. We wonder if there is someone or something else outside our world (God), but we don't know because we can't see out.

You would think that we'd be trying to figure out what's going on. But instead, most of us do nothing. When the BIG Stuff does come to mind, we usually don't talk about it or deal with it. It's like we'd rather spend our time in the hotel arcade or swimming pool or restaurant than go looking for answers.

Now, maybe you're not like most people. Maybe you ARE looking for answers. Maybe that's one of the reasons you're reading this book. If so...cool.

But most of us aren't like that. We don't deal the BIG Stuff. We just ignore it.

And we start to make excuses...

THE EXCUSES MUST DIE

Let me tell you a basic truth: I am not a fan of excuses.

Excuses are a huge cop-out that people use when they should just be dealing with their issues. So when I hear people giving excuses, I like to take them down. The excuses...not the people.

And that's what I'm about to do. I'm going to destroy your excuses.

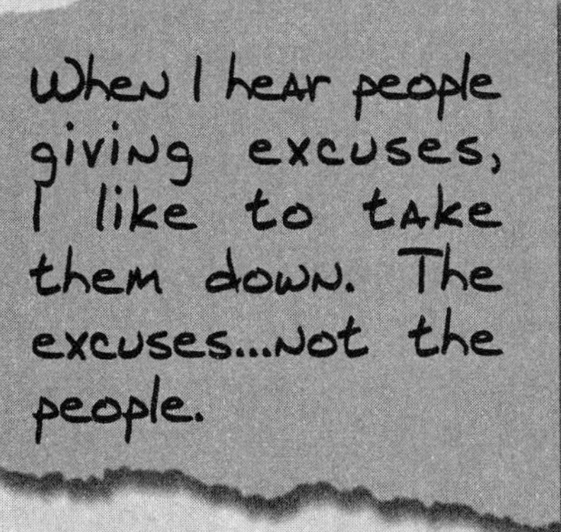

Why?

Because when I was riding that lawn mower every summer afternoon, I was just like so many people. I came up with excuse after excuse to avoid dealing with the stuff that mattered most.

But what I needed was a wake-up call. A smack in the face.

I needed someone to challenge me. Someone willing to look me in the eye and tell me how stupid it was to avoid dealing with the BIG Stuff. I needed someone to demolish all my excuses.

So that's what I am going to do now.

As I see it, there are four big excuses people give for ignoring the BIG Stuff. They may sound familiar. You may have used them at some point. I know I did. But after this...I promise they will be utterly obliterated and completely unusable.

So here we go...

EXCUSE #1 - "THE BIG STUFF DOESN'T MATTER"

BIG Stuff Example: LIFE

Have you ever walked to another room in your house to get something and then forgotten why you are there? You stop walking and think to yourself, "What was I supposed to get? Why did I come in here?" You know you had a reason for coming into the room. But you need to stop, and think, and figure out why you are there.

Have you ever done that? It happens to me all the time (maybe I took a few too many helmets to the head).

Well, most of us wouldn't get into the other room, forget why we are there...and then just sit down and turn on the TV.

But a lot of people live their whole lives like that. They know there might be a bigger meaning and purpose to life, but they don't think it's worth stopping to answer the question, "Why am I here on this earth?"

After all, there's school, work, practice, and homework to think about. There are friends to worry about. There are texts to answer, games to play, books to read, calls to make, and Facebook to check. People have a lot of things to get done every day, and that's the stuff that really matters.

Right?

TARGET: EXCUSE #1

Method of Destruction: REthink Your Strategy

Okay, let's be honest. Are you one of these people? Do you think the BIG Stuff might sound interesting, but it's just not that important?

If so, then you're confusing "what matters" with "what's next." The most important stuff may not be what is right in front of your face. You may need to take a step back and think.

Because, let's face it — our daily lives exist inside a bigger world, a bigger reality.

Every little detail of your life is like a piece in a 10,000-piece puzzle. Each one is a small part of the gigantic whole. And to make it all work together, you need to see beyond each little piece and get a bigger view. You need to see the picture on the front of the box in order to know how to sort out and understand all the little pieces.

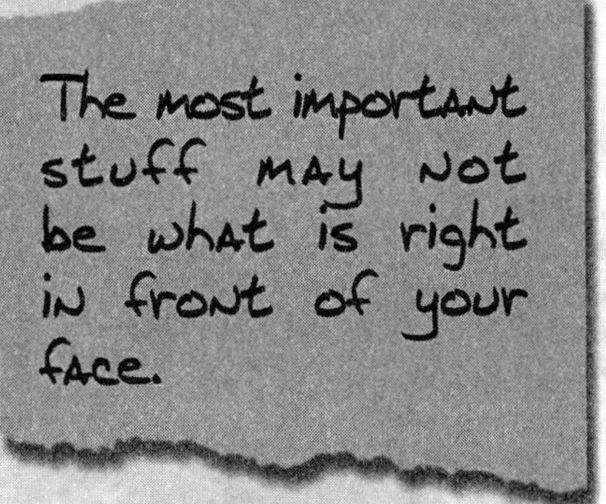

And that "picture" is the BIG Stuff.

The truth is...when you try to work from the little details, your life is chaos. But if you start by asking the big questions like, "Why am I here? What is my purpose?" and then work down to the details, everything else can fall into place.

Whether you want to believe it or not, to really navigate this life, you need a strategy that STARTS with the BIG Stuff.

Otherwise, you will never be able to make sense of all the details.

And that's why this excuse just doesn't work.

EXCUSE #2 - "THE BIG STUFF ISN'T URGENT"

BIG Stuff Example: Death

Excuse #2 is really just the Lie, rephrased a bit.

People who buy into this excuse don't deny that the BIG Stuff is important. They know it matters. But in their minds, it just doesn't matter RIGHT NOW.

After all, our days are filled with busyness, stress and multitasking. And, let's be honest, dealing with big questions does take time...time we just don't have.

So we put it off until tomorrow...and tomorrow...and tomorrow.

Maybe this is you. Have you ever thought, "This stuff is important. I should really take some time to deal with these issues." But that's as far as you get - a thought or a wish. You totally intend to figure all this stuff out. Just not right this minute.

But *will* you get to it?

Who knows? And that's my point.

TARGET: EXCUSE #2

Method of Destruction: REimagine the Possibilities

I have some news for you: RIGHT NOW is precisely when the BIG Stuff is important.

How do I know? Well, consider the possibilities.

First, you could live 80 more years on this earth. If that's the case, then you've got 80 years to make your life count. Get the BIG Stuff figured out. Find your purpose. Make your life worth something. But you only get one shot, so don't waste it. Start now and do something big. Because when your 80 years are up, you'll die and that's it.

Or second, you could die tomorrow...or third, at any random time in between.

But those are pretty much the possibilities. And in case you missed it, they all end the same way: you die.

Think about it...you could get hit by a bus. Or develop a brain tumor. Or choke on your breakfast cereal. You might run a red light. Maybe get shot in a convenience store robbery. It could even be a murder-for-hire by some psycho ex-girlfriend of yours.

The problem is, we don't know when it's going to be. I don't know. And neither do you. But it will happen. I assure you.

Of course, when you think about it, the real question isn't "When?" or "How?" The real question is "What happens next?" I mean, don't you ever wonder about that moment when your body stops living? Is it like sleep? Is there a bright light? Is there a soul, and where does it go?

And right about now, I can hear the heckling start: *"Okay, Joel, so this is this where you throw in the 'Heaven and Hell' stuff, right?"*

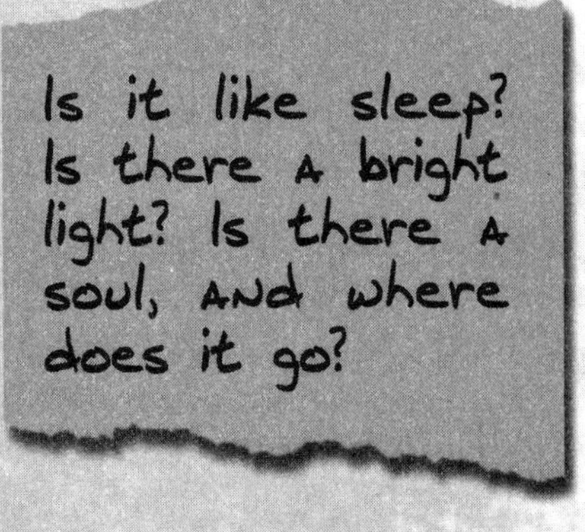

And my answer is...why not talk about Heaven and Hell? Is Heaven just harps and angels? Is Hell really so bad? Can I avoid Hell? How does someone get to Heaven?

You can't tell me that the stuff on your to-do list is really more urgent than figuring out what's going to happen after you die.

Because the truth is...the BIG Stuff is either so important that it can't wait...or it isn't BIG Stuff. If Life or Death or God could wait, then it would be no different than downloading the next big app for your phone or catching up on the stuff you've recorded on your DVR.

But the realities of Death and what happens after you die are too important to put off. Why? Because you could die! You may not have tomorrow. I may not have tomorrow. So when it comes to looking at the BIG Stuff, you can't just "get to it later." It demands attention now.

EXCUSE #3 - "THE BIG STUFF IS SCARY"

BIG Stuff Example: God

Some people are afraid of the big questions. And their fear shows up in three different ways.

1. Fear of the Unknown.

Let's be honest. Looking at the big picture is like looking down from a bungee-jump platform. Suddenly, it doesn't seem like such a good idea after all. These questions are really, really big. And worst of all...we don't know the answers.

There is no cheat sheet for the BIG Stuff. And that's frightening. When the BIG Stuff comes up, most people feel unsettled. So they push the thoughts down and instead fill their minds with smaller, less risky questions:

"Did you see American Idol last night?"
"Did you study for today's math test?"
"Are you going to the game on Friday?"

Of course, people know it's not the BIG Stuff...but at least they know the answers.

2. Fear of Conflict.

Some people are also afraid that the BIG Stuff is going to cause a fight. Because, truth be told, it probably will.

Now, don't get me wrong. I like an occasional in-your-face discussion. But I'm not most people. And the BIG Stuff has resulted in some serious conflict. Conflict that everyone would like to avoid at all costs (even me).

We've already talked about Life and Death. So now, let's throw God into the mix.

After all, it seems like the "God issue" is the one most likely to start something. Someone asks, "Does God exist?" And then the fists start flying: Which religion's take on God is right? Are God and Allah the same Person? How do Buddha, Mohammed, and Jesus figure in?

The problem is that we can't see outside this world — just like in that weird hotel without windows. We can't see out, but we've still got these questions. So everybody's got a guess, and everyone is sure that his answer is right. And since this is the BIG Stuff, and the answers really do matter, everyone is ready to fight to the death.

Actually, whole wars have been fought over these questions. Thousands, maybe millions, of people have died throughout human history because of how they answered these questions.[2] Families and friendships are totally destroyed over these issues. Talking about the BIG Stuff can lead to a lot of bitterness, hatred and judgment. And it just doesn't seem worth it.

People think that it's simply easier not to bring up the questions in the first place. They don't want it to get "all awkward" between friends. So they figure if they don't talk about it, then they can't fight about it.

Right?

3. Fear of Change.
Then, finally, there are the people who fear the BIG Stuff because it might mean rearranging the life they have so carefully constructed.

After all, if it's really BIG Stuff, then it's going to mean that their life has to change. They can't just do whatever they want. They are going to have to let go of their sense of control.

And...well...that's scary.

People don't want to change. They don't want to lose control. They're afraid some "God" out there is going to start making demands and ordering them to "start doing this" and "stop doing that." So they look the other way, hoping the BIG Stuff will just disappear, so they can go on with their lives.

TARGET: EXCUSE #3

Method of Destruction: REact Appropriately
Okay, I'm not gonna lie. This is the excuse I used the most when I was in school. I know it's kind of scary to consider diving into these big questions.

So I'm not telling you to just stop being afraid. But I AM telling you that your fear is not a good enough excuse to avoid the BIG Stuff. I'm saying...it's time to deal with your fear.

Okay, I'm not gonna lie. This is the excuse I used the most when I was in school.

And how you deal with it depends on whether you are more like Person A or Person B.

Imagine two people standing in a busy road with a bus coming straight for them. Person A jumps out of the way. Person B closes his eyes.

Guess which one gets hit by the bus.

It might be natural for you to be Person B, but whether it's a bus or the BIG Stuff, you cannot afford to just close your eyes.

On the lawn mower, I thought about the BIG Stuff almost every day. But I was Person B. I was scared, so I didn't deal with it. I just closed my eyes.

I should have been Person A. I should have realized how pointless it was to avoid dealing with issues out of fear. I should have told myself what I am about to tell you...

You're scared? Boo hoo. Get over it. It's time to face your fears.

EXCUSE #4 - "THE BIG STUFF IS RELATIVE"

BIG Stuff Example: Life, Death, & God

There is one final reason people give to avoid the BIG Stuff. And it's probably the most common one.

In fact, some of you are probably ready to put this book down right about now, aren't you? I can hear you rehearsing your issues already...

"Sorry, Joel...all this BIG Stuff talk sounds great. But I don't buy it. These questions don't have just one answer. What's true for one person may not be true for me, you know? You shouldn't push your answers on me, and I shouldn't push my answers on someone else."

Well, congratulations! You have just given Excuse #4.

You don't believe that there is just one right answer? Really?

Well...I'd like to challenge that thought. I think you do.

TARGET: EXCUSE #4

Method of Destruction: REmember Everyday Life

Let's say you have $17,000 in your bank account, and you decide one day that you want to withdraw it. You go to your bank and speak to the teller. "I'd like to withdraw all the money from my account," you say, "I have $17,000 in it, and I'd like it in cash."

She responds, "Actually, I don't believe you have $17,000 in that account; I believe you have $0." You firmly reply, "No, you're wrong. I want my money...now." But again she calmly replies, "Please do not push your beliefs on me. I don't like absolutes. You can believe there is $17,000 in the account; I can believe there is $0. There's not just one right answer."

We both know the teller is wrong. There is a right answer. And in everyday, practical life, you do believe in absolutes. You are either reading this book, or you are not. You're either sitting down right now, or you're not. The sky is either blue, or it isn't. We all live by absolutes everyday.

"But Joel, all this God stuff and Death stuff...it's not that simple. It's religion, and that's different."

Really? Why?

There is either a Heaven...or there isn't. There is either a God... or there isn't. Just because the issues are bigger doesn't mean you can pretend there aren't right answers.

In every area of your everyday life, you function as if absolutes exist. Which means that you cannot claim they don't exist in this area...just because you don't feel like talking about Life, Death or God.

It just doesn't work that way.

But there's an even bigger problem with this excuse: it doesn't make any sense.

Seriously, this whole idea completely contradicts itself. Someone who says, "There are no absolutes when it comes to religion" *is making* an absolute statement about religion. That's like me saying, "I can't speak English, not one word." The statement is self-contradictory. It's nonsense.[3]

This excuse is nothing more than an attempt to clutter the issue with smart-sounding ideas so you don't have to face the tough questions.

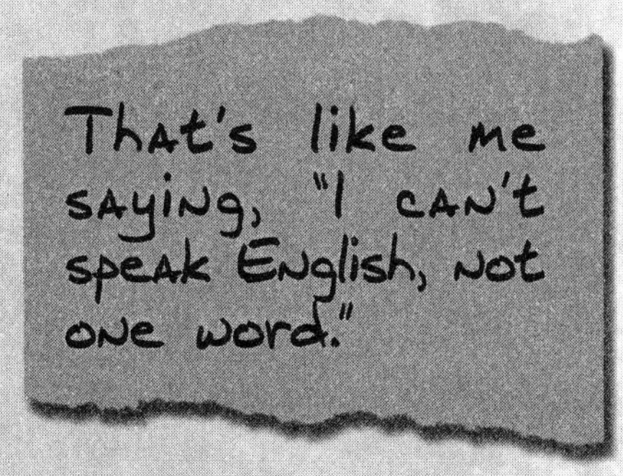

But no one gets a free pass because they claim they don't believe in absolutes. Whether you want to believe it or not, whether you buy it or not, the BIG Stuff is real, and you have to deal with the questions.

No excuses.

THE TRUTH

Life. Death. God. The BIG Stuff.

We have to deal with it. But let's be honest, thinking about those big questions is like being trapped in a hotel without windows. We aren't sure why we're here. We don't know what's outside. And we don't really have a clue what's coming next.

Which leaves us with a choice: do we just get through life, consumed by the details of our days? Or do we deal the really big questions that can give our lives real meaning and purpose?

I'd say it's time to take on the BIG Stuff.

Sure, we have lots of excuses for ignoring it. But our excuses are weak. Really weak.

That's why the whisper that "The BIG Stuff can wait" is a Lie.

We can't escape the realities of life. It just doesn't work that way. We have to deal with the BIG Stuff now. We have to face the questions head on. It's important. Really important.

Why? Because of what's at stake.

Let's take one last look at our Death issue just to prove my point. Maybe you would say, *"Dude, I just don't see the rush. I think there's maybe a 1% chance that Heaven and Hell even exist."*

Okay, well, let's talk about that 1% for a minute.

Let's say I hand you a cookie and tell you there's a 1% chance that you won't like it. Do you eat it? Of course...it's a cookie. Even if it's nasty, no big deal.

But let's say I hand you a cookie and tell you there's a 1% chance that it's poisoned and will kill you. Do you eat the cookie? Probably not. Even though the chance of poison is really small...well, your life is worth a lot to you.

Let's say I hand you a cookie and tell you there's a 1% chance that it's poisoned and will kill you.

Now let's talk about Heaven and Hell. Let's assume you're right that there's only a 1% chance they exist. But now we're talking about something bigger than a nasty cookie, something even bigger than your life. We're talking about forever.

In other words, when we are talking about the possibility of spending an infinite amount of time in either Heaven or Hell, we are talking about things that are infinitely important, no matter how skeptical you are.[1] You need to think this stuff through, NOW.

Refusing to consider the BIG Stuff is gambling with your forever. Do you really want to lose that bet?

You won't...if you find the right answers. Of course, there are a lot of possible answers out there. So how can you figure out which ones are true?

Well...that brings us to Lie #2.

MAKING IT PERSONAL

1. **Joel defines the BIG Stuff as Life, Death, and God. Do you agree that these three things are the biggest issues we face? Why or why not? Can you think of anything bigger?**

___

___

___

2. **Do you think that the BIG Stuff really matters in your everyday life? How does (or should) what you believe about Life, Death, and God affect the details of your days?**

___

___

___

3. **Excuse #2 says that the BIG Stuff isn't urgent. Do you agree? Why or why not?**

___

___

___

4. **When Joel mowed grass, he tried to avoid thinking about the BIG Stuff because it scared him not to have answers. Can you relate to his story? Have you ever avoided thinking or talking about the BIG Stuff out of fear (of the unknown, of conflict, or of change)?**

___

___

___

5. Do you agree that there really is absolute truth when it comes to the BIG Stuff? Why or why not?

___

___

___

6. Do you think it's worth the time and energy to try to deal with the BIG Stuff? Why or why not?

___

___

___

NOTES

1 As I look back, I don't think most of those people who taught me things in church were actually being fake. That is just how I saw it at the time.

2 I can't describe each of the wars that have been fought about God, but check out this website for a 90-second overview of religious conflicts all over the world: "History of Religion." Maps-of-War. 9 Sept. 2006. Web. 20 July 2011. mapsofwar.com.

3 Francis J. Beckwith, and Gregory Koukl. *Relativism: Feet Firmly Planted in Mid-Air* (Grand Rapids: Baker, 1998) 143-47.

4 Blaise Pascal. *Pascal's Pensees* (New York: Dutton, 1958) 52-58. His argument in this section is intended as "a letter to incite [the readers] to search after God." My goal is the same.

LIE #2:

"GOOGLE HAS ALL THE ANSWERS."

A Lesson From The Day I Didn't Wear Pants

All right, I admit it. I'm a motivational speaker.

I know, I know. I really hate that title. It makes me think of people who make whole schools play "Simon Says," who refer to high school students as "young people," and who say corny things like "Turn that frown upside down!" (I promise, I've never done any of those things.)

For a while I tried calling myself a "Teen Life Strategist." But after explaining what I did, people would usually say, "Oh, I get it. You're a motivational speaker!" So I guess I'm stuck with it.

But whatever you call me, I have the greatest job ever. Sure, traveling the country giving the same few talks over and over may sound boring. But it's not. It is anything but boring.

I once sat in traffic for five hours, wondering if I'd ever get to pee again. I've had to spend the night in the airport. I've rented a car that didn't start (more than once). I get the evil eye from locals pretty often (they can tell that I'm not from there), especially at small town pizza joints.

And what happens in the schools is even funnier. I've been introduced as Joe Pennington, Joey Pendleton and Joseph Henton. One time a female teacher volunteered to rap Vanilla Ice's *Ice*

Ice Baby in front of the student body. I'm not joking...you can watch the video at youtube.com/joelpenton. Three different times, a student has stood up and puked while I was speaking. I've even been expected to shout to a thousand students because the school didn't have any kind of sound system.

Still, I love my job. And it definitely has its perks. I've gotten free meals, free places to stay, and lots of free mugs, hats and t-shirts.

However, in my world, I have to depend a lot on other people. Usually people I've never met. And that can sometimes be, um, problematic...

For each event, a contact person fills out an online 'event information' form so I know what to expect. The form gives me details like how long to speak, the venue address, and appropriate attire.

One time the guy who filled out the form entered his home address instead of the venue address. On the night of the event, I showed up at his house, but no one was home. He was out of town...at the event where I was supposed to be. Nice.

And then there was the day I didn't wear pants.

I had been asked to speak at a leadership conference at a campground in southern Ohio. A guy named Jim filled out the online form several weeks in advance. I gave it a quick glance before I left. The description sounded like a standard student leadership conference. So I threw on my khaki shorts and collared shirt and made the drive.

This time, I did show up at the right place and at the right time. But I had a bigger problem: no students. This was a leadership conference for *adults*, hundreds of adults, all dressed in suits and ties!

I was met by Jim, my contact, and the president of the organization, a man at least twice my age. He shook my hand, slowly looked me up and down, and asked, "Do you need to go freshen up somewhere?"

"Nah...I'm good," I told him. I didn't have any other clothes with me.

As we walked to the auditorium, I wondered if I was crazy or just dumb. I checked Jim's form on my phone, this time more carefully. He had not specified that it was a conference for adults (so I'd assumed it was for students), and the field for appropriate dress had been left blank.

I gave my talk to a wide-eye audience, but despite their ties, they quickly loosened up. Afterwards, a guy told me, "I've been coming to this event for 30 years, and this is the first time I've seen anyone here in shorts...much less the main speaker!"

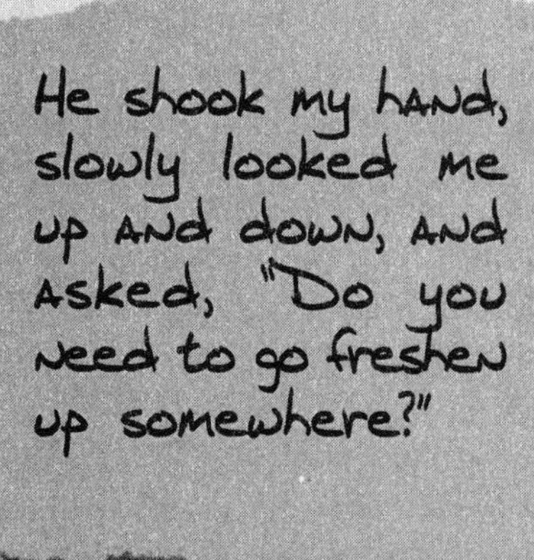

After that, I started following up with anyone who submits an incomplete event information form. Oh, and I also keep a few extra sets of clothes with me.

AN EVERYDAY LIE

Let's be honest. I learned a hugely important lesson that day: we need good sources.

Everyday, we get information from lots of sources. But which ones can we trust?

Well, sometimes, it's easier to know which ones NOT to trust. Like those magazines on the rack in the grocery store line. You know the ones I mean. They have stories like these:

"Alien Mummy Goes on Rampage"
"Vegan Vampire Attacks Trees"
"Woman Delivers Own Baby While Skydiving!"

Obviously, these are the tabloids. So we don't give them much credit. Right? It doesn't take a genius to know that you shouldn't get your news from the tabloids.

So what does this have to do with Lie #2?

Simple. The BIG Stuff. We have all these questions about Life, Death and God. But we need more than a list of questions. We need the answers.

And Lie #2 doesn't want to keep you from asking the questions. It just wants you to go to the wrong source for your answers... which could lead to disaster.

Think about Jim, my contact for the leadership conference that summer. I went to the form he completed to answer my question about what to wear. But he left out that answer. So the form was definitely not a good source. And I ended up seriously under-dressed.

But this chapter isn't about pants. It's about the BIG Stuff. And that means finding a good source is even more important when you consider what's at stake (see Lie #1).

Lie #2 says that you can find your answers to the BIG Stuff in the same places that we find the answers to all our other questions. It says that our "normal" sources should work just fine.

But the problem is...our normal sources won't work just fine. They aren't good enough. And I can prove it.

Just think about the three sources we typically use...

Lie #2 says that you can find your answers to the BIG Stuff in the same places that we find the answers to all our other questions.

Source #1 - The Collection
Many eons ago (okay, more like 25 years), people searched for answers in books, like encyclopedias. Biology report on monkeys due tomorrow? See volume "M" of the World Book Encyclopedia sitting on the shelf in the high school library.

I know...sounds horrible.

Thankfully, we now have a much better option: the Internet.

When we need information on monkeys (or money or Mel Gibson or Miss Universe or the melting point of aluminum)... when we want to know the top news, see the latest viral video, or check out the latest blog...when we're wondering who won last night's game...we simply Google, and the answers we want instantly appear before us.

But, books still exist. And the magazines and newspapers are all still available, too. I know this because I see people reading them at airports when I travel. (Those people are usually old.)

And together, these sources pretty much put at our fingertips the general information to get us through our daily lives, our science classes, and our sports/music/celebrity/funny YouTube video addictions. If you need basic information about someone, something, or some place...it's been written down somewhere. You just have to find it.

Source #2 - The Community
But sometimes we need answers to more personal questions. And in that case, the Internet (or books and magazines) really won't help.

What if you want to know, "Should I go out with her?" Or, "What should I major in?" Maybe "Should I apologize for throwing up on my sister?" is your question. Or you're wondering (like I did in the sixth grade), "Would it be weird if I drove my riding lawn mower to school?"

When these are the issues we're trying to find answers to, we almost always turn to Option #2: the Community. In other words, our friends and family. We go to the ones who know us best when we have questions that we can't or don't want to answer on our own.

The Community can be a really great resource. Your friends and family know who you are and where you've come from. They've walked through your struggles and triumphs with you. They know your personality and your habits and your preferences.

So when you need advice, you turn to them. And for some topics, that works out okay. (By the way, yes, you should apologize for throwing up on anyone, even if it is your sister. And yes, it would be really weird to drive a lawn mower to school.)

Source #3 - The Center
Of course, even your friends and family don't have the answers to all your questions. So that brings us to Option #3.

When you need general information, you can find a book or website that will tell you what you need to know. Your friends and family can tell you what they think you should do. But when it comes to what you really WANT to do, the best option is to stick to the most simple plan: look inside.

This is, of course, what most of us do, most of the time.

We look inside ourselves for the answers for lots of questions. Do I love her? Will this job fulfill me? How can I be happy? Should I order fries with my burger? And if it "feels right," we figure it probably is right.

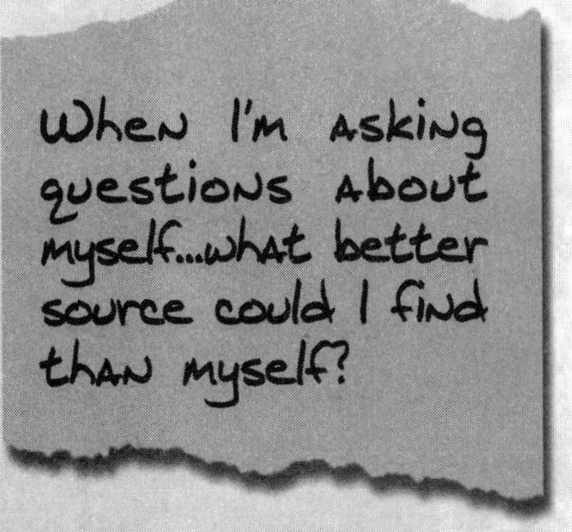

After all, when I'm asking questions about myself... what better source could I find than myself?

STUCK INSIDE

Unfortunately, there is a problem. All three of our usual sources have one major flaw when it comes to the BIG Stuff.

They are trying to answer OUTSIDE questions from the INSIDE.

Okay...just go with me for a minute here.

We live in the physical world. And our three sources come from that world, too. So we can generally trust those sources for questions about the physical world and the lives we lead inside that system. We can go to the Collection for general facts. We can go to the Community for personal advice, and we can go to the Center to find our own desires. And for the most part, the answers we get will work.

But...what if our questions have to do with something OUTSIDE our system?

Think back to the hotel without windows from Lie #1. The hotel is full of people just living their lives. But they are all in the same situation as you are. They are all locked inside, too.

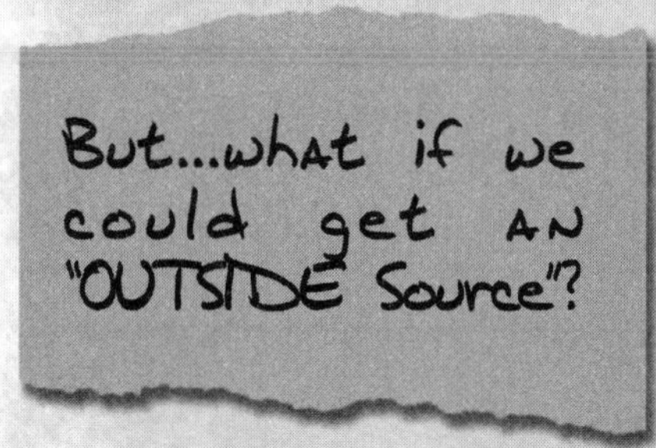

If you want to know how to function inside the hotel, then you are in great shape. You can ask anyone you meet there, and they can tell you what you want to know.

But if you ask them why you are in that hotel or where the disappearing people go or what's outside...well, they can't see anything more than you can see. So their answers are no better than anything you can come up with yourself. They are trying to answer OUTSIDE questions from the INSIDE.

And that's exactly the same problem we have with the BIG Stuff.

Questions like, "What's the meaning of life? What happens when you die? Is there a God?" go beyond the physical world. Those questions go beyond general facts, personal advice and our own desires. Those questions are above every person, place and thing on earth. They are completely OUTSIDE our system.

So our typical sources just won't work. Whether you look for answers in yourself or from people close to you, or from a million weirdos on the Internet, they are still answers from mankind. A mankind that's stuck INSIDE the system.

But...what if we could get an "OUTSIDE Source"?

What if you were sitting in the lobby of that hotel, wondering what exists on the other side of the locked door, when you notice something on the floor. It's a scrap of paper, barely showing at the bottom of the door. You pull it inside to discover that it's a note. From someone outside.

And suddenly...things are different. Suddenly...you might have some real answers. Suddenly...you're in business.

"Come on, Joel...an OUTSIDE Source? Notes under a door? What are you talking about?"

Hang on for just a little bit longer...it's time to play a game.

THE GAME: "WHAT IF..."

What if there is a God?

I know a lot of people don't think there is. Some people don't think it's very cool to believe in God. Some of the "really smart" people say he's just a fictional being created by people who can't survive by themselves. They say the whole concept of God is a crutch, an excuse, an attempt to escape the realities of life.

But...is it?

What if we don't rule out the possibility that there is a God? What if we keep that option open just for a minute? Think about it.

What if there is a God?

Of course, you can't prove his existence (no one can). On the other hand, you can't prove that he doesn't exist either. Again, no one can. So that means his presence is a legitimate possibility. It's possible that God does exist. And it would be stupid to eliminate God as a possible source to answer our questions simply because we don't want to consider his existence in the first place.

It's like someone who refuses to try a new food or drink because he might not like it. I have a friend who will not try fish because it might taste "fishy." She's not allergic to fish, but she's still not willing to risk the "bad" flavor she thinks the fish will have. And there are a lot of people out there, just like my friend. They rule out a legitimate possibility (that they will like it) simply because they don't want to risk not liking it. That's just dumb.

Now, obviously the existence of God is a lot more significant than trying fish at some restaurant. But the idea is the same. It's just not rational to rule out a legitimate possibility (God exists) for no real reason.

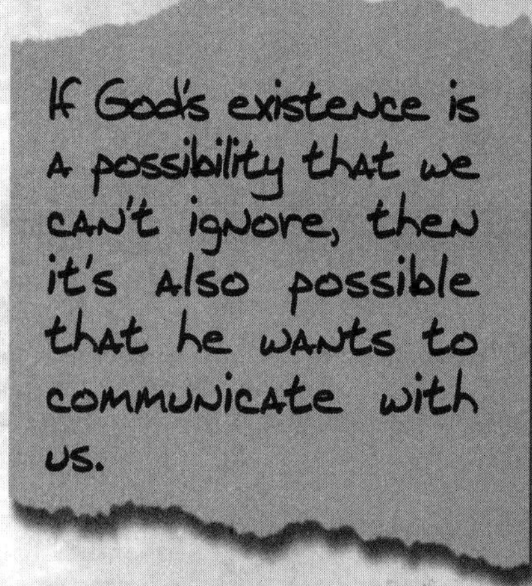

And think about it...if there is a God, wouldn't He make a good source? He would certainly qualify as an OUTSIDE Source. So, just for a second, go with me...

What if there is a God... *and* He slipped us a note under the door? What if He actually did give us answers from the outside? If God's existence is a possibility that we can't ignore, then it's also possible that he wants to communicate with us.

A VOICE FROM HEAVEN?

Of course, now we have another problem. Sure, there might be a God out there who wants to say something to us. But just think of all the stuff in our world that claims to be from God.

There's lots of it.

People all over claim to have "heard God speak" to them. And every major religion (and some minor ones) have a sacred book that is supposedly inspired by God. Muslims have the Koran, Hindus have the Vedas, Christians have the Bible, and on and on and on.

But with all this stuff that claims to be from God...how can we know which, if any, of the claims are true?

Well, we could just say they're all from God (like some people think). Or we could say that none of them are from God (like some other people think). But those are just cop-outs people use so they don't have to really think through the issue.

Remember...our only hope of getting answers about the BIG Stuff is to find an OUTSIDE Source, so we need to be willing to work a bit on this one. We need to do some testing and see which options, if any, actually stand up to scrutiny.

So I propose three tests. Three qualities that something from outside our system should have. An OUTSIDE Source, one that could really have come from God, should be all three of these things:

1. Credible
2. Incredible
3. Impactful

Think about it. If some source claims to be from God, but can't get its historical facts straight, it isn't *credible*. So we throw it out. If the information is really from God, it had better do something that goes above and beyond human abilities; it needs to be *incredible*. And if something comes from God himself...it had better be *impactful*. It should have a major effect on the world.

As far as I'm concerned, if any of the information out there passes these three tests, we will have found a viable option. We will

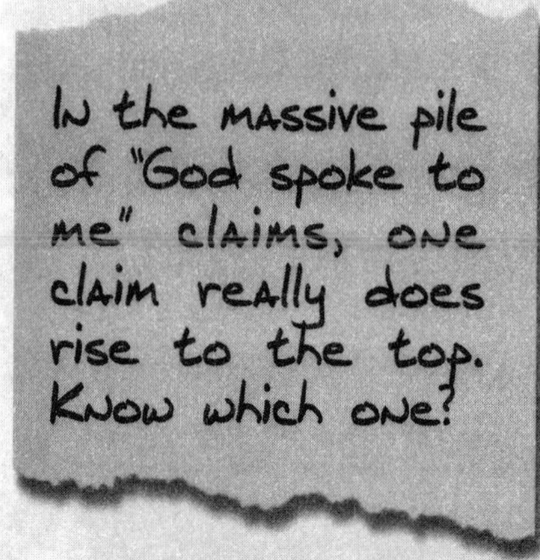

have found a source that might actually be from God...from the OUTSIDE.

Now, I don't have time or space to actually do these tests myself here. And thankfully, I don't have to. Lots of people who are lots smarter than I am have done them for me. You can go look it up, just like I did.

But you know what they found, all those super-smart people? When you put all those religious claims to the test, one really does stand out. In the massive pile of "God spoke to me" claims, one claim really does rise to the top.

Know which one? The Bible.

Now, I can sense your complete lack of surprise at my conclusion. I can hear some of you out there already starting to rip me apart...

"Of course you think it's the Bible, Joel. You're one of those Christian Bible lovers. What else would you say?"

Well, don't worry. It's not about what I say. I don't expect (or want) you to take my word for it. I want you to actually look at the facts with me. And when we're done, it should be clear that the Bible really is the most likely option to be that "note slipped under the door" that we so desperately need if we are going to figure out the BIG Stuff.

So here we go...

THE TESTS

1. The "Credible" Test

I have some shocking news for you. The Bible was written a long time ago.

Okay, so that's not really shocking. Most people have figured that one out on their own. But it's still important. Know why?

Well, do you remember the Telephone Game? A message gets passed from person to person, and by the time it gets to the end of the line, the message sounds NOTHING like the original, right?

Well, the same thing can happen with books, especially old ones.

The longer a book has been around, the more chance it has of getting messed up. A word could get changed. A sentence rewritten. Whole sections get edited or deleted or...well, messed up. Until, after centuries of changes, the book is nothing like the original. It's actually a huge concern.

So, smart guys came up with a test to check for accuracy of old books. It's called the Bibliographic Test. (And no, you don't have to remember that.)

The Bibliographic Test factors in two things:

1. The amount of time that separates the original and the oldest copies. Less time = less chance for mistakes to have been made.

2. The number of available hand-written copies for a particular book. More copies = more ability to compare and fix any discrepancies.[1]

"Okay, can you give me some examples?"

Well, take Plato. He was a Greek philosopher who wrote about 400 BC. The oldest manuscripts we have of his writings are dated 900 AD. That's a 1300 year difference! And we only have a total of 7 manuscripts.

Then there's Homer's *Iliad.* He's a lot better off than Plato. There's only a 400 year difference between the copies and the original. And we have 643 copies. For an ancient text, that's fantastic![2]

And as for the Bible, get this...only about 225 years separates the originals and the copies of the New Testament. (Some fragments of copies are as close as 50 years!) And there are over 5,300 copies. 5,300![3]

The Bible passes the Bibliographic Test at the top of its class. It easily blows out of the water ALL other ancient texts, religious or not.[4]

But accuracy is only one area of the Credibility Test. Let's look at a second area: archaeology.

Lots of these old texts claim to be historically accurate, the Bible included. But most people assume the Bible is just a bunch of stories with made-up names and places and battles and stuff.

"So who's right? Have archaeologists dug up any evidence that either supports or discredits the Bible's claims?"

Um...yeah. They've actually found lots of stuff. One good example is King David.

According to the Bible, David was one of the greatest kings of Israel.[5] He captured Jerusalem by sending his men through a well called the Pool of Siloam.[6] And he was a poet; he wrote most of the songs that make up the largest book in the Bible, Psalms.[7]

The problem is, for a long time, historians totally disagreed. They didn't think David even existed. They were also pretty sure the Pool of Siloam was outside the city walls of Jerusalem (thus making it useless for an invading army). And they believed the Psalms were not old enough for David to have written them.[8]

That's what historians thought until recently when...

1. Pottery inscribed with "House of David" was found dating from the time the Bible says David lived.[9]

2. Archaeologists realized that the ancient walls of Jerusalem did extend beyond the Pool of Siloam.[10]

3. They unearthed proof that the music in the Psalms could actually date back to the time of David.[11]

The problem is, for a long time, historians totally disagreed. They didn't think David even existed.

Of course, that's just a few examples. But they're not the only ones. Lots of archaeological evidence has been unearthed (literally) that proves story after story in the Bible.[12]

Still, many people don't want to admit that the Bible is credible. They throw test after test at it, trying to disprove and discredit it, like some ridiculous teacher who writes all his tests to flunk the A student. But the Bible, like the A student, aces every test.

The truth is, no trustworthy archaeological find has EVER contradicted the Bible.[13] In fact, archaeological evidence consistently shows that the Bible is every bit as credible as any other ancient text.[14]

So the Bible passes the Credibility Test...but there are still two more tests.

2. The "Incredible" Test

Well, we need our source to be credible. But more than that, we need it to be *in*-credible.

We need something that can do more than our regular sources can do. Something out of this world.

We need something...miraculous.

Think about it. Something is miraculous if it is not bound by natural laws like gravity. It's super-natural. Above nature. OUTSIDE of nature. And that's exactly what we need. A source that does more than is naturally possible. That would be pretty incredible, wouldn't it?

Yes, it would. So the question is, "Is the Bible in anyway miraculous?"

Um...how about regularly (and correctly) predicting the future? I'd say that's pretty miraculous.

Check it out.

In 700 BC, a guy named Isaiah predicted the fall of Babylon.[15] The Babylonian empire fell to the Persians in 539 BC.[16] Over 150 years later.

Isaiah also said that a Persian king named Cyrus would rebuild Jerusalem.[17] But the funny thing is that he predicted that 100 years before Jerusalem was destroyed in the first place.[18] Oh... and wouldn't you know, the first king of the Persian Empire was a guy named Cyrus[19]...who rebuilt Jerusalem shortly after taking the throne.[20]

So, Isaiah seems to know his stuff. But there are literally hundreds of other examples. Here are a few more...just for fun...

The Bible also recorded

...that Babylon would destroy Israel (Jeremiah, chapter 25), which it did.[21]

...that Alexander the Great would rule and his kingdom would be divided in four parts after his death (Daniel, chapter 8), which is exactly what happened.[22]

...and that Rome would destroy Jerusalem (Luke, chapter 19), which happened in 70 AD.[23]

Without a doubt, the Bible has an insanely accurate record for predicting the course of human events. In other words, it seems to have an "out of this world" ability to tell us what's going to happen before it does. And that's a talent that no other ancient text seems to have.[24]

Which makes the Bible pretty incredible.

3. The "Impactful" Test

Okay, so the Bible seems to pass the Credible Test. And the Incredible Test.

But some of these random "God spoke to me" claims can sound credible. And they can definitely seem to be incredible.

So we need one more. One more test that can't be cheated, can't be fixed, can't be fooled.

We need one more. One more test that can't be cheated, can't be fixed, can't be fooled.

The message had better be impactful.

If God himself, the One who created everything, is really giving us answers, I'm not going to believe it unless the message makes a huge impact on the world. Let's face it. If some source is just pretending to be from the outside, its answers are going to fall flat. They just won't work.

But if the source is really "slipped under the door," it will make a tsunami-size impact. And no claim has ever made a bigger impact on the world than the Bible. Not even close.

Think about it.

No other book has been more bought, sold, or given away. The Bible is the best-selling book EVER.[25]

No other book had been more widely read, memorized or quoted. It's been translated into over 2,200 languages.[26] I didn't even know there were that many languages on Earth until I read that statistic. *The Diary of Anne Frank* and the *Harry Potter* books have only been translated into 60 or so languages each.[27] So the Bible is well ahead of the game.

No other book has been more thought about, talked about, or written about.[28]

No other book has had more hospitals, schools, or governments founded on its principles.[29]

The fact is...no other book has had the worldwide impact that the Bible has had. Period.[30]

SO WHAT? NOW WHAT?

Okay, so according to these facts (seriously, they are facts — feel free to look them up), what have we proven?

Well...let's be honest. They don't *prove* that the Bible is from God.

But they do show that the Bible is in a class by itself. And if there ever was a "note slipped under the door," then the Bible has to be the leading contender. When all the other "God spoke to me" claims are compared to the Bible, they fall far, far short.

And that means that the Bible is unique. So we should check it out.

Think about it. We would get really annoyed with a friend who refused to see a really great movie just because he didn't feel like it. He would be an idiot to miss out on a cutting-edge, record-breaking, visually amazing movie for no good reason.

If there ever was a "note slipped under the door," then the Bible has to be the leading contender.

So...

If we really do want answers to the BIG Stuff, we would be idiots to ignore a book that is so credible, so incredible, and so impactful. It would be ridiculous to have a source like this as an option...and never even look into what it says.

Even if you aren't convinced that the Bible is from God...fine. Even if you're not sure there is a God...doesn't matter. Based on its credentials, the Bible is still the best shot we have at an OUTSIDE Source. And that means that we need to check out what it says before we toss it out the window once and for all.[31]

Which brings us to an obvious question...what does the Bible say?

WHAT THE BIBLE SAYS (AND DOESN'T SAY)

Well...let me begin with what the Bible doesn't say.

See, a lot of people don't want to consider the Bible as a good source for the BIG Stuff because they think it's just a long list of rules that are meant to make us all miserable.

I have good news. The Bible is NOT a list of dos and don'ts. Seriously.

Okay, so there are some rules in there. Don't murder.[32] Don't steal.[33] Don't trip blind people on purpose.[34] That stuff IS in there.

But that stuff is not the whole picture. Actually, contrary to popular belief, the rules are just a small portion of what the Bible has to say.[35]

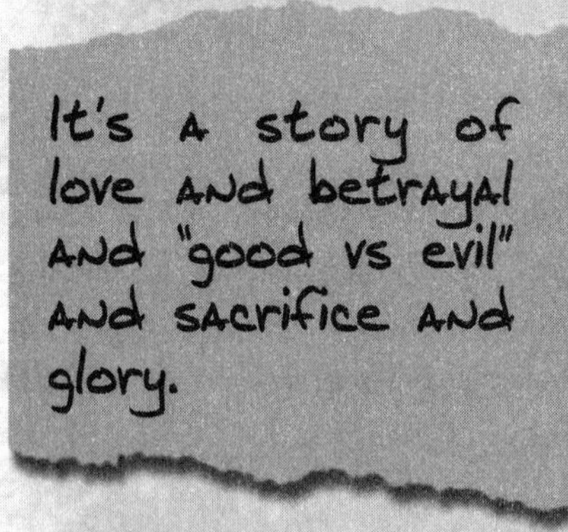

See, according to the Bible, God didn't want to just give you rules to follow. He wanted to tell you a story. A true story. A real story. It is the story of God and mankind. It's a story of love and betrayal and "good vs evil" and sacrifice and glory. And it's a story that offers us answers to the BIG Stuff.

THE TRUTH

Lie #2 wants you to think that Google and your parents and your heart are good enough sources for all your questions, including the BIG Stuff.

And for a bunch of people stuck inside a hotel without windows, that whisper can sound pretty good. But Lie #2 is wrong. They aren't good enough. They are INSIDE sources. And our questions are too big for them.

What we need is a note slipped under the door. In other words, we need an OUTSIDE Source.

And I suggest we look to the Bible for our answers to the BIG Stuff.

Why the Bible? Because the Bible, more than any other possible source, passes our three tests.

- It's Credible. The Bible is historically and factually consistent.
- It's Incredible. The Bible's ability to predict future events is absolutely miraculous.
- It's Impactful. More than any other book, the Bible has made a real difference in the lives of people in every time and place.

And so, for the rest of this book, we are going to check out God's story. We're going to see what answers the Bible actually offers. If it's the best option as an OUTSIDE Source (and it seems to be), then we need to start there.

So, let's get some answers...starting with Lie #3.

MAKING IT PERSONAL

1. Have you ever found yourself in an embarrassing situation because you trusted something that you shouldn't have? What happened?

___

___

___

2. Joel listed three primary sources that we use to find answers to our question (the Collection, the Community, and the Center). What do you see as the biggest benefits and problems with each source?

___

___

___

3. When thinking about Source #3 (the Center), would you say that "if it feels right, it probably is right"? Why or why not?

___

___

___

4. Do you agree with Joel's claim that we can't answer the BIG Stuff using "inside-the-system" sources?

___

___

___

5. **What facts about the Bible did you think were the most important for passing each of the three tests for an OUTSIDE Source (Credible, Incredible, and Impactful)? Which ones did not persuade you?**

____

____

____

6. **Do you generally believe the Bible is just a list of rules or something more? Why?**

____

____

____

NOTES

1 Josh McDowell. *The New Evidence That Demands a Verdict.* Rev. ed. (Nashville: T. Nelson, 1999) 33-34.

2 McDowell, *New Evidence*, 37-38. The chart here proves just how fantastic those numbers are! And as Greenlee notes (pg. 37), since scholars consider the secular texts trustworthy, even with so little evidence, the Bible can also be considered reliable.

3 McDowell, *New Evidence*, 34-40.

4 McDowell, *New Evidence*, 37-38. Bruce notes that "no body of ancient literature...enjoys such a wealth of good textual attestation as the New Testament." And Zacharias concludes, "There is nothing in ancient manuscript evidence to match such textual availability and integrity."

5 1 Chronicles 11:9 - *And David became greater and greater, for the LORD of hosts was with him.*

6 2 Samuel 5:8 - *And David said on that day, "Whoever would strike the Jebusites, let him get up the water shaft to attack 'the lame and the blind,' who are hated by David's soul." Therefore it is said, "The blind and the lame shall not come into the house."* Also, Norman Geisler. Baker Encyclopedia of Christian Apologetics (Grand Rapids: Baker, 1999) 51.

7 Of the 150 Psalms, seventy-three are attributed to David. See Carol L. Meyers. "Psalms, Book of." World Book Advanced. World Book, 2011. Web. 20 July 2011.

8 Geisler, 51.

9 "Tel Dan Stele." Wikipedia, The Free Encyclopedia, 1 July 2011. Web. 20 July 2011. Also, Hallvard Hagelia. "THE FIRST DISSERTATION ON THE TEL DAN INSCRIPTION." *SJOT: Scandinavian Journal of the Old Testament 18.1 (2004): 136.*

10 Geisler, 51.

11 Geisler, 51.

12 Geisler, 48-52.

13 Geisler, 52. "While thousands of finds...support in broad outline and often in detail the biblical picture, not one incontrovertible find has ever contradicted the Bible."

[14] Josh McDowell. *The Best of Josh McDowell: A Ready Defense.* Comp. Bill Wilson. (Nashville: T. Nelson, 1993) 68. "If one discards the Bible as being unreliable, then one must discard almost all literature of antiquity." Also, McDowell, *Best of,* 115. "Archaeology...does, however, put the one who wishes to maintain the traditional view on at least an equal footing with the skeptics."

[15] Isaiah 13:1–11 - *The oracle concerning Babylon which Isaiah the son of Amoz saw. On a bare hill raise a signal; cry aloud to them; wave the hand for them to enter the gates of the nobles. I myself have commanded my consecrated ones, and have summoned my mighty men to execute my anger, my proudly exulting ones. The sound of a tumult is on the mountains as of a great multitude! The sound of an uproar of kingdoms, of nations gathering together! The LORD of hosts is mustering a host for battle. They come from a distant land, from the end of the heavens, the LORD and the weapons of his indignation, to destroy the whole land. Wail, for the day of the LORD is near; as destruction from the Almighty it will come! Therefore all hands will be feeble, and every human heart will melt. They will be dismayed: pangs and agony will seize them; they will be in anguish like a woman in labor. They will look aghast at one another; their faces will be aflame. Behold, the day of the LORD comes, cruel, with wrath and fierce anger, to make the land a desolation and to destroy its sinners from it. For the stars of the heavens and their constellations will not give their light; the sun will be dark at its rising, and the moon will not shed its light. I will punish the world for its evil, and the wicked for their iniquity; I will put an end to the pomp of the arrogant, and lay low the pompous pride of the ruthless.*

[16] Seth F. C. Richardson. "Babylon." *World Book Advanced.* World Book, 2011. Web. 20 July 2011.

[17] Isaiah 44:28 - *who says of Cyrus, 'He is my shepherd, and he shall fulfill all my purpose'; saying of Jerusalem, 'She shall be built,' and of the temple, 'Your foundation shall be laid.'"*

[18] Geisler, 613. Also, Jonathan Mendilow. "Jerusalem." *World Book Advanced.* World Book, 2011. Web. 20 July 2011.

[19] 2 Chronicles 36:22 - *Now in the first year of Cyrus king of Persia, that the word of the LORD by the mouth of Jeremiah might be fulfilled, the LORD stirred up the spirit of Cyrus king of Persia, so that he made a proclamation throughout all his kingdom and also put it in writing.*

[20] Geisler, 613.

[21] Richardson, "Babylon."

[22] Roisman, Joseph. "Alexander the Great." *World Book Advanced.* World Book, 2011. Web. 20 July 2011.

[23] Mendilow, "Jerusalem."

[24] McDowell, *New Evidence*, 13. Geisler and Nix comment that "other books claim divine inspiration, such as the Koran, the Book of Mormon, and parts of the [Hindu] Veda. But none of those books contains predictive prophecy." Also Geisler, 615, where Foster notes, "There is not a single one of them [the oracles of heathenism] that meets the tests required to prove supernatural agency, which every Scripture prophecy evinces."

[25] McDowell, *New Evidence*, 8.

[26] McDowell, *New Evidence*, 8-9.

[27] "The Diary of a Young Girl." Wikipedia, The Free Encyclopedia, 7 Jul. 2011. Web. 20 Jul. 2011. Also, "Harry Potter in Translation." Wikipedia, The Free Encyclopedia, 20 July 2011. Web. 20 July 2011.

[28] McDowell, *New Evidence*, 14-16. Ramm notes, "No other book in all human history has in turn inspired the writing of so many books as the Bible."

[29] McDowell, *New Evidence*, 17. Grady Davis says that "it [the Bible] has been the most available, familiar, and dependable source and arbiter of intellectual, moral, and spiritual ideals in the West." And Sivan comments, "The Bible has given strength to the freedom fighter and new heart to the persecuted, a blueprint to the social reformer and inspiration to the writer and artist."

[30] McDowell, *New Evidence*, 15-16. Some would say that the Bible has also had a negative impact on the world because it has been contorted to support things like the Crusades and the Slave trade. This doesn't demonstrate that the Bible is inherently bad. It just further illustrates that the Bible is powerful. A stick of dynamite can be used to liberate trapped miners as well as blow up a building of people. The way people use it will determine the type of impact, but the impact it has will always be big.

[31] McDowell, *New Evidence*, 16.

[32] Exodus 20:13 - *You shall not murder.*

[33] Exodus 20:15 - *You shall not steal.*

[34] Leviticus 19:14 - *You shall not curse the deaf or put a stumbling block before the blind, but you shall fear your God: I am the LORD.*

[35] Five of the sixty-six books that make up the Bible are considered to be "law" though even the rules in those books are set within a narrative.

LIE #3:

"IT'S ALL GOOD."

A Lesson From My Junior High Football Coach

In 7th grade, I played football for Lincoln Junior High School in Van Wert, OH.

Now, if you know anything about me, you know that I was not good at sports as a kid. Seriously not good. I was always one of the last to get picked...if I was picked at all. I dropped nearly every ball that came my way. I couldn't throw to save my life. I was really, really bad.

Thankfully, I got better along the way. But as a seventh grader, things hadn't improved yet. I still wasn't very strong or coordinated. And my team was pretty bad, too.

Well, that's not exactly true. My team was...well, horrible. That year, we were 0-5 going into the last game of the season.

But being bad wasn't a big deal to us. We were used to losing. For us, it was so normal that we stood on the sidelines, joking around and making fun of each other. Watching our sidelines, you wouldn't even get the vibe that we sucked.

Then came the last game of the season.

We were playing our rivals, the Celina Bulldogs. But it wasn't much of a competition. We were getting killed. Like, seriously blown out. I'm talking 36-0...at halftime. It was pathetic.

But as usual, it was also no big deal. At halftime, we were in the locker room, joking around. Suddenly, our coach flung the door open and came in. His face was bright red, and he was breathing hard. We stopped laughing. We stopped talking. We just sat there, silent.

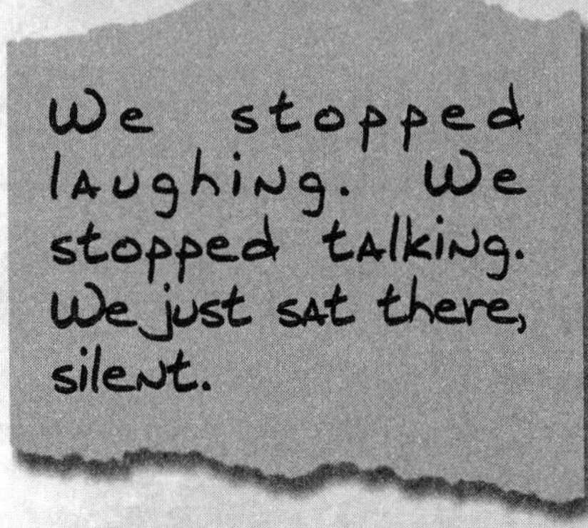

My coach, on the other hand, was anything but quiet. "What is going on with you guys? What is wrong with you? Don't you care at all? Can't you read the scoreboard?"

I kept my head down, hoping he wouldn't single me out.

He yelled, "How can you guys act like this when we are getting killed?" And then...he really went off. With a loud thud, he kicked a helmet. It sailed across the room, slamming even more loudly into a locker just above my friend Drew's head.

"Wow," I thought, "He almost bashed Drew's face in with a helmet...he must be serious."

He stormed back out of the room, and we just sat there. We took the field after halftime and finished the game. We lost.

That night, I thought about the game and what the coach had said. Maybe he was just being negative. Everyone else was so positive and encouraging. Wasn't it important to just enjoy playing the game? Should we really care that much what the scoreboard says?

What was the big deal?

AN EVERYDAY LIE

My junior high football coach taught me a valuable lesson that day.[1]

We thought things were fine. Sure, we lost a few games. Sure, we had a horrible record for the season. Sure, koala bears could have played better than we did that year. But we still thought we were fine.

Why?

Because nobody was acting like it was a big deal. My teammates, our parents, our friends...they were all saying that the score didn't matter. As long as we were doing our best, it was all okay. It was enough that we had tried.

And then my coach kicked a helmet. And I came face to face with Lie #3.

So what is Lie #3?

Basically, it's the little whispers all around you that everything is okay. You are okay, people are okay, there's no need to freak out. No matter how things seem, you don't have to worry because, "It's all good."

But my coach understood the truth. Things were not "all good." Things were really, really bad. And it took that helmet slamming into a locker to make me realize how wrong we really were. We were terrible. And we had been suckered into believing Lie #3.

"Joel, where are you going with this?"

I'm going to do for you what my coach did for me that day (without kicking a helmet, of course). I'm going to tell you the truth.

See, Lie #3 is everywhere, every day. It's not just something that seventh grade football players believe. It's the line you're getting fed from radio DJs, politicians, your boyfriend, TV commercials and all sorts of other sources. Everywhere you turn, someone is going to be telling you that things are okay.

But the truth is...things are not all good. The truth is...things are very, very wrong. The truth is...we have a very big problem.

THE PROBLEM

"So what's the problem?"

The problem is that our situation is just as messed up as my seventh-grade football team. It's halftime, and a quick glance at the scoreboard tells the sad, sad story.

We're losing. Badly.

I mean, let's be honest...the world is pretty jacked up. Poverty. Crime. War. You get the picture. You watch the news. Or someone you know does.

There's no question, our world is a mess. Everywhere you look, things are broken, and nothing we try seems to fix anything. No matter how many politicians we elect, or wars we fight, or laws we enact, or petitions we sign, things just don't seem to get any better. In fact, we often make it worse.[2] Without a doubt...all is NOT well in our world.

> I can see the sun shining. I can hear the birds chirping. I can taste the delicious Cold Stone "Cake Batter" ice cream.

Now maybe you think that I'm just too pessimistic. Maybe you see the world as a good place.

Well, don't get me wrong...I can see the sun shining. I can hear the birds chirping. I can taste the delicious Cold Stone "Cake Batter" ice cream. I know there is good stuff in the world.

But I also know that more than 800,000 people were murdered in about 100 days during the 1994 Rwandan Genocide.[3]

If you can't see that the world is also filled with pain, suffering and all sorts of evil...if you can't admit that something has gone very wrong here, then you've been blinded. You've bought into Lie #3, and you need to open your eyes.

And you know what? It's not just the world as a whole that is broken. Individuals are just as jacked up.

So many of those people we'd call "successful," those people we would expect to have it all together? Money and fame haven't fixed their lives. Celebrities are in and out of rehab all the time. Sports stars keep getting arrested. Former millionaires are standing in unemployment lines.

The "average" person isn't doing so well, either. Families are falling apart. That single mom can't pay her bills. The head cheerleader has an eating disorder. The "smart" kid in your math class has been cheating on tests for years.

No matter how good we look on the outside...the truth is, people are broken. All of us. You. Me. Your next-door neighbor. Your teacher. The King of Norway. And all the nameless people who pass by us every day.

I know this because I hear it from students all the time. Recently a girl who I'll call Katie sent me the following message on Facebook:

> *"Joel, in fourth grade I started cutting my arms with scissors. When my parents found out, they hid all the blades in the house but I still pinched, bit, scratched and stuck tacks in my arms. Anything that would transfer the emotional pain to physical pain. Lately, I have*

been doing a lot better but my best friend just committed suicide and I don't know what I'm going to do. Please help me."

It's time to face reality - things are pretty bad.

Could they be worse? Sure. But, if we are honest with ourselves, we have to admit that we're all a wreck. We're lonely. Empty. Overwhelmed. Tired. Desperate for happiness. Longing for direction.

Sometimes life sails smoothly along. But deep down...something isn't right. No matter how good it looks, our lives are totally broken.

There just isn't any other way to say it.

THE SOURCE

"Well...thanks, Joel, for the recap on how much life sucks. It's been a blast. Is that it? 'Cause if it is, I'm going to watch some YouTube videos."

Don't worry...that's not it. If that's all I had to say...well, we're both wasting our time. I'm not about just pointing out the problems and heading home. I want a solution. I want to talk about how to get things going in the right direction.

And that means we have to start with a big question...WHY?

"So why are things totally messed up?"

Well...I'm not going to tell you. No, really. I'm not.

See, I don't want to waste your time with just my thoughts on all this stuff. After all, we're talking about the BIG Stuff, and I'm stuck in humanity just like everybody else (see Lie #2). No...it's time to check out an OUTSIDE Source (see Lie #2 again).

It's time to check out what the Bible has to say.

And that means, I want to let the Bible speak for itself. Not just me telling you what the Bible says, but actually looking together at the text.

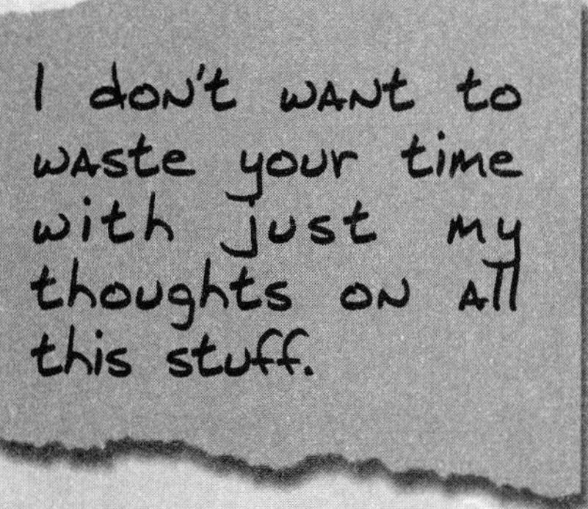

Of course, you'll still hear a lot from me in the rest of this book. But when trying to figure out BIG Stuff, I'll always start with the Bible.

And to help with that...here's what we'll do:

- Each of the next five chapters will focus on the Bible's actual words. We'll take a whole section, a chunk of maybe 1-2 paragraphs. And then we'll break it down, a little at a time.
- The Bible's text will always be in a different font so it's immediately clear which words are from the passage and which words are just my ideas.
- Try to read the passage slowly and maybe more than once. Really think about what it's saying.
- Keep in mind the Bible was written a long time ago so the style may be difficult to read. If you don't get the point, that's okay. Keep reading. I'll try to explain stuff that may not make sense right away. But don't just take my word for what the Bible means. Check my ideas against the actual text. That's the important stuff.

All right. Here we go...

THE ROOT OF THE PROBLEM

The Bible says that the brokenness we see in our world and in ourselves is the result of one fundamental problem. It all has to do with how we relate to God.

Check it out:

> For the wrath of God is revealed from heaven against all ungodliness and unrighteousness of men, who by their unrighteousness suppress the truth. For what can be known about God is plain to them, because God has shown it to them. For his invisible attributes, namely, his eternal power and divine nature, have been clearly perceived, ever since the creation of the world, in the things that have been made. So they are without excuse. For although they knew God, they did not honor him as God or give thanks to him, but they became futile in their thinking, and their foolish hearts were darkened. Claiming to be wise, they became fools, and exchanged the glory of the immortal God for images resembling mortal man and birds and animals and creeping things. (Romans 1:18–23)

Now, I know, that's a pretty big chunk of heavy stuff. But it's hugely important. So feel free to read it again. Slowly.

All right, now we're going to start breaking it down. But it will help if I first tell you a story...it's the story I share in schools all over the country.

MY FRIENDS

When I was in middle school and high school, I had a group of close friends. We did everything together. Sports. Classes.

Hanging out on the weekends. All of it. These guys had been my best friends for years.

And then something changed. Instead of hanging with us, one of the guys went partying on a Saturday night. And the next weekend, he took another one of the guys with him. And then another. One by one, they all drifted into the party scene.

Everyone but me.

I wasn't into partying. I knew that it could mess up my goals on the football field. So they went. And I stayed. And for a while, it worked. Sort of.

"No problem," I figured. "We'll be okay. We can still be friends."

But I was wrong.

Why? Because they didn't just do different things, they started thinking differently, too. They assumed that, "Joel won't drink with us, so he must think he's better than us." And in their minds, their "right" to party was more valuable than our friendship.

So, one weekend, when I showed up at the house where they were hanging out, they wouldn't let me in. I was no longer welcome.

I felt so alone. So left out. So betrayed.

"How could they do this?" I wondered. "How could they all just drop me like that? Maybe they'll change their minds."

But they didn't. They were done with me. I lost every last one of my best friends that night. They abandoned me over some beer and a few weekend parties. I was deeply hurt. I was totally confused.

And I was pretty angry, too.

Getting betrayed is one of the worst experiences in life.

THE CONNECTION

Now...maybe you've been betrayed, too. Maybe you know exactly how I felt. And maybe you're wondering what that story has to do with our passage from the Bible. Actually, it has everything to do with it.

Look at my story again.

My high school friends ditched me because they started believing things that weren't really true. First about partying (that it was okay) and then about me (that I thought I was better than them). They convinced themselves that they were right, and because I refused to go along with their new way of thinking, they ditched me.

And I got angry. Which, to be honest, makes me a big, fat HYPOCRITE.

Why? Because I am guilty of the same thing...only worse.

My friends deceived themselves, and as a result, they betrayed me, which sucks.

BUT...according to the Bible passage, I have deceived myself, and as a result, I betrayed the Creator of the Universe!

I got angry. Which, to be honest, makes me a big, fat HYPOCRITE.

And guess what? So have you.

"Okay, you must not be talking to me now. This part is probably for other people."

Wrong. I AM talking to you. I'm talking to each and every person on the planet.

We have all deceived ourselves and betrayed God. And it is that self-deception and betrayal that is at the very foundation of all that is wrong with the world.

Sound crazy? Well, that's what the Bible says…let's start to break this passage down.

THE DECEPTION

The whole problem starts with self-deception. And it's self-deception that leads to betrayal.

Here, read it for yourself...

> **For the wrath of God is revealed from heaven against all ungodliness and unrighteousness of men, who by their unrighteousness suppress the truth.**

Okay, so the Bible doesn't actually use the term "self-deception." Instead, the Bible says we **suppress the truth**.

"So...what does that mean?"

Well, the idea of **suppress** is pretty simple. It means "to hold something back" or "to hold something down."

It's like this. Have you ever been around a seriously dysfunctional person? You know, someone who gets upset about things but never talks about anything. They just bottle up their anger. They do this for so long and are so good at it that they don't even realize they are angry at all. Psychologists make a lot of money off of these people.

That person is **suppressing** their anger. They are bottling it up inside and not letting it emerge.

And the Bible says what we are **suppressing** is **the truth**. It's there, but it's being bottled up.

The Bible is saying that we are, inside our own hearts and minds, pushing **the truth** down, holding it back, refusing to let it emerge. Inside ourselves, we have **the truth** tied up; we've ignored it, denied it, pushed it back and down so much that we don't even realize it's there anymore. We are subconsciously deceiving ourselves.

We've ignored it, denied it, pushed it back and down so much that we don't even realize it's there anymore. We are subconsciously deceiving ourselves.

All of us have done this. You. Me. Everyone. And as a result, God is very angry (**the wrath of God is revealed**).

As He should be.

PLAIN AND CLEAR

"Oh, come on, Joel. God is really mad because I'm "suppressing truth"? What truth? Seriously, I don't even know what you're talking about!"

Well, actually, you do. That's what the Bible says anyway. Check out the next verse:

> For **what can be known about God is plain to them**, because **God has shown it to them**.

Whether you think you have ignored **the truth** or not doesn't really matter. You have. So has every other person on earth.

And **the truth** that we are holding back is huge. It's massively important.

It's the truth about who God is.

And, according to the Bible, it's plain to see. The truth isn't hidden or fuzzy. This is the basic, obvious, right-in-front-of-our-eyes kind of stuff that God has shown to all mankind.

"Like what kind of stuff that's so obvious to see?"

Well, there are at least two things about God that are plain and clear. They're in the next verse...

> For his invisible attributes, namely, his eternal power and divine nature, have been clearly perceived, ever since the creation of the world, in the things that have been made. So they are without excuse.

So what are they? Simple...

1. God's eternal power. In the world around us, God displays His unending, timeless power. His ability to accomplish what He's got planned.

2. God's divine nature. Basically, that's the parts of God that make Him God. It's His supernatural nature.

And the Bible says that we can see those qualities in the world around us. We can't see God. He's invisible. But His power and God-like qualities are on display all around us.

It's kind of like our hotel. We're inside. There are no windows, and the doors are locked. We don't know what's outside.

But at the same time...the hotel is there.

Someone had to make the hotel. Hotels don't just appear out of nowhere, right? So the fact that there even is a hotel is a huge indication that there is Someone outside the hotel with the power and resources to build it.[4]

And by looking at the hotel, we can make some assumptions about Who's outside. The hotel is complex, with lots of rooms and floors. So Whoever built it was smart, a good designer. The whole system (like the plumbing and lights) works together, so the Builder prefers order and organization.[5]

We can't see the Someone who built the hotel. He's invisible to us. But we can learn some things about Him just by looking around.

We can't see the Someone who built the hotel. He's invisible to us. But we can learn some things about Him just by looking around. That's what the Bible is talking about here. We can easily look around and see who our Creator is in His creation. **The truth** about God is, literally, as **plain** as day.

And because **the truth** is so obvious (**clearly perceived**), we have no excuse if we choose to ignore it (**they are without excuse**).

WHAT SHOULD HAVE BEEN

Next, the Bible gives us a quick glimpse at how we should have responded to **the truth** about God.

> **For although they knew God, they did not honor him as God or give thanks to him.**

So it looks like we should have done (but didn't do) two very important things:

1. We didn't **honor** God.
2. We didn't **thank** God.

"Why should we honor and thank God?"

Because that is the only thing that makes sense based on **the truth** we see about Him in creation.

Okay...think of it this way...let's say you find a diamond buried in your back yard. And you notice two things about the diamond:

1. It's massive. The thing is huge, nearly the size of your fist.

2. It's flawless. You get it checked out and you know...it's clear, it's pure, and it's definitely not fake. This thing is legit.

Based on those two qualities, you can conclude something very important. Your diamond is precious. It is surely one of the most valuable stones in the world.

And what do you DO with your diamond? I'll tell you exactly what you do...you treasure it. You keep it safe and admire its beauty (at least until you find a billionaire who's willing to buy it). Basically, you treat it in way that is fitting with its value.

And THAT is where we went wrong with God. We saw **the truth** of His **eternal power** and **divine nature**. It would only make sense that we would find Him so precious and valuable and worthy that we would **honor** Him and **thank** Him.

There is actually a word for this. When we treat something like it is of the highest worth, it's called worship. We should have recognized that God is so worthy that we would worship Him.

But we didn't.

God should have been our greatest treasure.

But He wasn't.

We suppressed the truth of how valuable He is.

We deceived ourselves, and it started us down the road of betraying the Creator of the Universe.

FULL BLOWN BETRAYAL

Now, I know this is getting a little heavy and maybe a little depressing, but keep going with me for a minute.

Think about my friends again.

They didn't just stop treating me like their friend. It's not like they just didn't invite me to a birthday party. They actually wouldn't let me in the house to hang out. They intentionally, purposely, completely rejected me.

And what we did to God was infinitely worse.

We didn't just forget to say grace over a meal here and there. That's not what the Bible is talking about. And it's not just that we turned away from Him. It's that we turned away from Him...TO something else.

Look at the next verse:

> They...exchanged the glory of the immortal God for images resembling mortal man and birds and animals and creeping things

In other words, we replaced God.

Think about your diamond again. You treasure it. You know its worth. But let's say you start deceiving yourself into thinking that the diamond isn't valuable at all. So you stop treasuring your diamond as you should.

Now along comes some random guy on the street selling plastic bead necklaces. For some reason you convince yourself that the plastic beads are worth more than your diamond. So you trade away your diamond (which is priceless) for some stupid fake jewelry (which is worthless).[6] That's dumb.

> For some reason you convince yourself that the plastic beads are worth more than your diamond.

Well, we took what we had (**the glory of the immortal God**) and traded Him in for something far less valuable (**images resembling mortal man and birds and animals and creeping things**).

We swapped the REAL God for FAKE gods. We **exchanged** the Creator for created things. And we thought that we had made a fair trade. We actually thought we got something better than God.

Now why did we do that? Because WE are dumb.

No, really. That's what the Bible says. Look again at the passage:

> **but they became futile in their thinking, and their foolish hearts were darkened. Claiming to be wise, they became fools**

We have these really good brains, but we aren't doing anything good with them (**futile in their thinking**). When we thought we were being so smart...we were really doing the dumbest thing possible (**became fools**).

We had the REAL God, the greatest treasure in all the Universe. But in our stupidity, we traded Him in for FAKE gods.

We deceived ourselves and betrayed God.

No wonder He's angry.

A GLANCE IN THE MIRROR

"But Joel, all that stuff...didn't it happen like thousands of years ago? Why is God mad at me for their stupid choice?"

Because nothing has changed. We still value the creation more than our Creator.

"Seriously, Joel. I'm not an idiot. I know that birds aren't God. So I don't really have a problem. I'm willing to say that God is God."

It's not about saying God is God. It's about treating God like He is God. Valuing Him above everything else as your greatest treasure. It is about worship.

I don't care who you are. Everyone has a greatest treasure, something they value more than everything else in the world. Maybe it's an actual person. A boyfriend or girlfriend. Maybe your dad. Maybe your best friend.

I don't care who you are. Everyone has a greatest treasure, something they value more than everything else in the world.

But maybe it's not a someone. Maybe it's a something. And you worship that something with everything that is in you.[7]

Let me give you some examples...

Image

Is image your FAKE god? Maybe you are totally consumed with what other people think about you. You might completely rearrange your life and the things you wear, watch, do and say just so people will think you are cool.

Is this you?

Maybe you think the most valuable thing in the world is fitting in. So you will do anything to be accepted by a particular person or particular group.

Do you think that being embarrassed in front of lots of people is the very worst thing that could happen?

This is why celebrities have people to manage their "image," to make sure that people think they are one way...even if they are totally different in reality. And while most of us don't have "public relations" people to help us with our image, we do ANYTHING and EVERYTHING to make sure that no one thinks we're a loser.

That's worship.

Friends

Are your friends your FAKE gods? Maybe it's not what everyone thinks about you that drives you, but your friends' approval is the most important.

You might find yourself going to movies you don't want to see or parties you don't enjoy because that's what your friends are doing. You just do whatever your friends think is cool at the time. You just agree with whatever your friends say.

Maybe you are scared to THINK differently, SPEAK differently, or ACT differently because if you do, you might lose your friends.

That's worship.

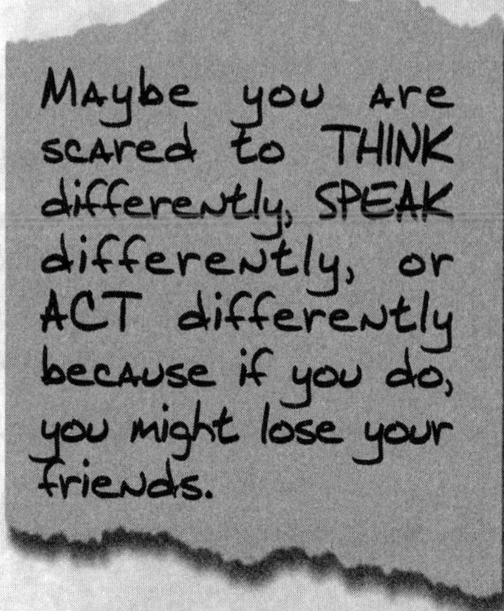

Achievement
Is achievement your FAKE god? It might not matter what route you choose...but whatever it is...you just have to be the best.

You might turn everything into a competition. Because you know you will win. And you just love that feeling more than anything. It doesn't matter how much work it takes. Or how much time. Or what you might have to sacrifice. You must succeed. You just have to win.

Maybe your greatest fear is failure.

Ever been totally destroyed because you got a B on a test? Ever been depressed for a week because you dropped what would have been the game-winning catch? Have you refused to take a part in the school play because you didn't get the lead?

That's worship.

Experiences
Are experiences your FAKE gods? You might be absolutely consumed with getting that next rush. And you will do anything to get it.

Maybe it's video games,
Or sex,
Or shopping,
Or drugs,
Or concerts,
Or eating,

Or sports,
Or partying,
Or whatever.

You just want to escape. And when you get your fix, all the other cares in the world are gone. Nothing else matters when you feel good. So you just live for that next experience. And the next. And the next.

> You just want to escape. And when you get your fix, all the other cares in the world are gone.

That's worship.

Celebrity
Is celebrity your FAKE god? Maybe famous people or fame itself is the most important thing in your eyes.

Do you have pictures of celebrities plastered all over your bedroom walls? Do you ever try to copy what certain actors or actresses are wearing or doing? Do you know more about your favorite sports team than your own sister? Would you just about kill to have your picture taken with Justin Timberlake?

What would you do if your favorite musician walked in the room right now? Would you be in awe?

That's worship.

So, there's my list. Of course, that's not a complete list, obviously. We all worship lots of things. These are just the most common ones. But, there's actually one more I want to mention. It's the mother of all FAKE gods. This one underlies all others. In fact, I would go so far as to say that EVERYONE worships this FAKE god...

Self

Is self your FAKE god? Maybe the most important person in the world is you. Maybe the most important thing in the world is getting what you want. It's all about your desires, your hopes, your dreams.

Want to know why you immediately look for the picture of yourself when you get your school year book?[8] Or why it bugs you that your little sister gets so much attention? Why you get so mad when someone cuts you off in traffic? Or why you hope no one grabs that corner piece of cake before you get to it?

It's because you worship yourself.

Of course, we do, occasionally, think about other people. We know it's good to do nice things for the world around us, especially at Christmas time. But let's be honest...why do we really do those things? Probably to feel good about ourselves.

You might not even realize it, but...deep down...your biggest concern and your number one priority is YOU.

That's worship.

THE TRUTH

So we have a problem...with worship. It's not that we don't worship. It's that we worship the wrong thing.

It's like we are sitting in the lobby of that hotel without windows (see Lie #1), reading the note that got slipped under the door (see Lie #2). We're looking for answers. And we're hoping for some really good news.

But instead, what we get is very, very bad news.

Because, according to the Bible, WE locked the hotel door. Once upon a time, that door was open; we **knew** the Creator. We **knew** the REAL God. But then we did something really, really dumb.

We deceived ourselves by treasuring the hotel (FAKE gods) more than we treasured the One who built it (the REAL God).

So we slammed the door in God's face (we betrayed Him). We locked ourselves inside. And we threw away the key.

Now all is NOT well. And it's all our fault. The world is backwards because we've gotten the most important thing backwards: our relationship with God. We worship creation instead of our Creator.

And when we make ourselves and people and things the highest priority in our lives, it reveals that we have ALL deceived ourselves and betrayed God. Which means that we really are fools. Fools with a really big problem:

God is ticked.

So we need to get things straightened out.

"But how, Joel?"

We have to get back in touch with the REAL God.

If our decision to turn away from God is the problem, then the solution must be to ditch all the FAKE gods we worship and turn back to the REAL God. No more replacements...no more FAKES.

If our decision to turn away from God is the problem, then the solution must be to ditch all the FAKE gods we worship and turn back to the REAL God.

So...now it's time to get real. What do YOU think? Where are you with all that I've said? Do you think I'm crazy? Do you see my point? Are you ready to turn away from these FAKE gods and turn to the one true God? Are you almost there but not quite? Do you think I'm on crack?

Whatever you think right now, let's keep moving. We gotta figure out who this REAL God is.

On to Lie #4...

MAKING IT PERSONAL

1. Do you agree that this world and the people in it are "jacked up"? Why or why not?

2. Have you ever been betrayed? How did that situation make you feel? What did you do about it?

3. In this chapter, Joel claims that self-deception can lead to betrayal. Do you agree? How does the Bible passage from this chapter say people deceive themselves about God?

4. What images come to mind when you hear the word "worship"? How do those ideas match the concept of worship portrayed in our passage?

5. **Think of the FAKE gods that Joel mentioned at the end of this chapter. Would you add anything to the list? What?**

____

____

____

6. **Every person, even Christians, struggle with worshiping FAKE gods. Which of the FAKE gods from the chapter (or others) do you tend to worship?**

____

____

____

NOTES

1 I know that the proper term is "koalas," not "koala bears." I used koala bears because it sounds funnier.

2 Our technological advances, policies and elected officials often make matters worse. Despite all our technological and industrial advancements, we've discovered, as Winston Churchill noted in a Convocation address at MIT, "that what has been called the Century of the Common Man would witness as its outstanding feature more common men killing each other with greater facilities than any other five centuries together in the history of the world." Winston Churchill. "MIT Mid-Century Convocation." 31 March 1949. MIT, 1999. Web. 20 July 2011.

3 Timothy Longman. "Rwanda." *World Book Advanced.* World Book, 2011. Web. 20 July 2011.

4 J.P. Moreland. *Scaling the Secular City: A Defense of Christianity* (Grand Rapids: Baker, 1987) 17.

5 Moreland, 43-47.

6 John Piper. *The First Dark Exchange: Idolatry.* 4 Oct. 1998. Desiring-God, 2011. Web. 20 July 2011. This sermon on Romans 1:20-23 helped me understand and illustrate this concept.

7 Timothy Keller. *Counterfeit Gods: The Empty Promises of Money, Sex, and Power, and the Only Hope that Matters* (Google eBook. New York: Dutton, 2009. Web. 20 July 2011) xiii-xvii.

8 I have heard DA Carson use this example several times. I can't remember exactly where it came from, but I wanted to make sure he got the credit for this idea.

LIE #4:

"GOD IS AN UN-STUFFED TEDDY BEAR."

A Lesson From My Cluelessness

I spoke recently at a charity event in Columbus, Ohio. It went pretty well. At least until we were done.

That's when I did something really stupid.

See, my job wasn't just to speak. Afterwards, I was supposed to stand at a table, answer questions and accept donations if people wanted to give to the charity. So that's what I did.

I was chatting with some people when this guy came up to shake my hand. He was a short, normal-looking guy wearing jeans and a brown coat. He said, "I really appreciate all that you do. I will send you a donation in the mail."

Now, I've done this a while. I'm no dummy. So, even though I heard his words clearly, what it sounded like to me was this: "Right now I feel like making a donation because I'm looking you in the face, but when I go home, I will definitely forget because it's really not that important to me."

Yep, sounds mean, doesn't it? But that's what I thought. Why? Because that's what happens...a lot.

And because a lot of people do that, I keep a stack of stamped, already-addressed envelopes right there on the table. But this guy didn't grab one. So as he was heading out the door, I rudely shouted, "Well, at least take an envelope!" (Mean, again...I know.)

Suddenly everyone around me got kind of quiet. It seemed strange, but I have a pretty loud voice, so I figured my voice had caught their attention.

He shouted back, "Oh, I'll be able to find you!" And everyone standing around me laughed! Now I was totally confused, but, fortunately for me, he left just seconds later.

As soon as the door closed behind him, the guy working the table with me looked at me with wide eyes and said, "Joel! Don't you know who that was!?"

> The guy working the table with me looked at me with wide eyes and said, "Joel! Don't you know who that was!?"

Obviously, I didn't.

"That was the Governor of Ohio!"

Oh man. I immediately got that feeling in my stomach. You know the feeling, like I was in the principal's office or being pulled over by a cop. I thought, "He didn't look 'special' at all. He didn't have bodyguards or expensive-looking clothes. He just looked normal." I mean, I don't really watch the news. So how was I supposed to know?

Amazingly, he came back just a few minutes later and said, "Actually, I will take that envelope." I smiled as I handed it to him and said, "Here you go...Sir."

My friend laughed at me and the situation. I was just glad I got a chance to redeem myself. And thankfully, I didn't mess up too badly because, a few weeks later, he did mail in a donation.

But I think I just got lucky.[1]

MADE TO ORDER

So, maybe that story makes you think I'm a jerk. Or an idiot. Well, I may not be extremely nice or the smartest person on the planet, but I do have a point. I promise.

Here it is: Our perception of a person has nothing to do with who that person really is.

I figured this pretty normal looking guy at my charity event was just what he looked like...a normal guy. But he wasn't. He was a big shot. He was in charge of my entire state. Every day, he made decisions that impact millions of people...including me.

But since he wasn't wearing a name tag that said "Governor of Ohio," I assumed he wasn't important. It was a huge mistake. And I was totally embarrassed.

But amazingly, it's the same mistake that lots of people make every day. Not about some politician, of course.

About God.

See, we go through life thinking that how we view God determines who He is. It's a lot like those Build-A-Bear stores. Maybe you've heard of them.

The concept is pretty simple. Little kids go in and pick an un-stuffed animal. Then they get to add their own stuffing, sounds, clothes and props. Finally, they give it a name and get a birth certificate.

One kid wants a soft pink leopard bear that says, "You're the best!" and wears a tutu and ballet slippers. Done. Maybe another kid wants a nice firm brown bear who wears hard-core motorcycle apparel and says, "Let's go!" Easy. Basically, each kid can create a new "best friend."

So what's my problem with Build-A-Bear? Absolutely nothing.

But I do have a problem when the Build-A-Bear mindset starts showing up outside those bright yellow mall storefronts. When it begins to seep into our fundamental way of thinking.

When it turns into Lie #4.

What is Lie #4? Simple. It's the concept that we can create our own version of God...our very own Build-A-God. Made to order. And it appears almost every time religion comes up in conversation.

Just think about it.

I meet people all the time who think it's fine to be a mostly-Buddhist who also likes to quote a few of Jesus' best one-liners. And how often do people say that you don't have to accept the entire Bible...you can just pick out the stuff you really like? Or what about all the people who want you to "keep an open mind"?

A whole lot of people believe Lie #4. But...it's totally wrong.

Here's the truth — God is not who YOU say He is. God is who HE says He is.

We cannot create our own versions of God to worship. We have to worship HIM alone. And if we want to worship the REAL God, then we have to start by figuring out who He is.

If we want to worship the REAL God, then we have to start by figuring out who He is.

Why? Because if we don't...well, we'll do some pretty stupid things. Just like I did. I didn't recognize the Governor of Ohio, and I acted like an idiot. But when we don't recognize God or if we treat Him like He's less than who He is, well, that's infinitely more stupid, don't you think?

"So how do we find out who God says HE is?"

You know this answer. We turn to our OUTSIDE Source, the Bible.

BRUCE WAYNE IS A COPYCAT

Of course, before we get to the Bible, I'd like to talk about Batman.

I love the *Batman* movies. And one of my favorites is *Batman Begins.* In the movie, a young Bruce Wayne is the richest guy around with every luxury a human could want...but there's a problem.

He looks around and sees that the world is completely broken. So he decides to do something about it.

He goes on a mission. A mission to change the world.

He trades in his designer jacket for a homeless man's coat. In reality, he's wealthy beyond measure, but he gives it all up. He gives up his name and his celebrity, and he becomes a nobody. He becomes poor. Sure, he could access his money at any moment. But he doesn't.

He sees the mission through and returns from his journey to retake his place of honor and wealth.

Great story. Too bad it's a copy.

Those Batman writers stole that idea from God.

Let me show you...

> **who, though he was in the form of God, did not count equality with God a thing to be grasped,**

> but made himself nothing, taking the form of a servant, being born in the likeness of men. And being found in human form, he humbled himself by becoming obedient to the point of death, even death on a cross. Therefore God has highly exalted him and bestowed on him the name that is above every name, so that at the name of Jesus every knee should bow, in heaven and on earth and under the earth, and every tongue confess that Jesus Christ is Lord, to the glory of God the Father. (Philippians 2:6–11)

"Huh?"

Yeah, it sounds a little weird and academic. But those strange-sounding phrases actually describe something mind-blowing.

That section tells the story of how God went on a mission to save the world. Kind of like Bruce Wayne (that copycat).

Let's break it down.

STAGE ONE: PRE-MISSION

A quick look around creation tells us that the Creator is rich. God owns everything and lacks nothing. He is powerful and divine (see Lie #3).

But more than that, God actually invaded humanity as a person named Jesus.[2]

So, according to the Bible, if you want to know who the REAL God is, you have to look at Jesus.[3] And what does the Bible say about Jesus? We'll, let's start here:

> he was in <u>the form of God</u>,

Simply put...Jesus is God.

The verse says Jesus was in **the form of God**. It could have also said the "essence of God." Or the "substance of God."[4] It's like saying a tree is in **the form** of wood. The substance of a tree is wood.

That means Jesus is the REAL God. Not a god. He's the One and Only God. Not one of many. He's it. Not just a nice guy. Not just a prophet. Jesus is God. Period.

And actually, the Bible says the same thing in other places, too.

- John called Jesus "**the only God, who is at the Father s side**" (**John 1:18**).
- Paul called Jesus "**God overall**" (**Romans 9:5**).
- Thomas called Jesus "**my Lord and my God**" (**John 20:28**).
- Peter called Jesus "**our God and Savior Jesus Christ**" (**2 Peter 1:1**).

The real Jesus, the One that the Bible talks about...He's God – in the flesh! And because He's God...the entire universe is His. He made it.[5] He owns it.[6] He rules over it.[7] Jesus is the King.[8]

But this King had a mission to complete...

STAGE TWO: THE DESCENT

Next, the Bible tells us that God didn't just sit back in luxury while the world He created destroyed itself.

Instead, He set out to fix this broken world. He didn't just hang out on His throne in Heaven. He got down off his throne and got His hands dirty.

> **he did not count equality with God a thing to be grasped, but made himself nothing, taking the form of a servant, being born in the likeness of men.**

Like Bruce Wayne leaving his riches behind, in a single amazing move, God left His throne. He left behind the glory that was His.[9]

The Bible describes it in these ways:

- Jesus could have held on to (**grasped**) his rights as God, but He chose to let them go.
- Jesus could have kept everything, but He **made himself nothing**.
- Jesus could have been served, but He chose to become **a servant**.

Instead of leaving His creation to suffer from our brokenness, God chose to identify with us by coming to Earth as one of us. He was literally **born in the likeness of men**.

In other words, God became a man. It's not that He stopped being God. Somehow, amazingly, Jesus is fully God and fully human.[10] At the same time.

> Like Bruce Wayne leaving his riches behind, in a single amazing move, God left His throne.

And the God-man stepped into our world.

But he didn't come in the way we would expect God to come, as a powerful political figure or an influential businessman. Like most babies born on this planet, Jesus' birth went almost unnoticed.[11] His parents were nobodies.[12] He came from an average family in a small town.[13] (It probably had only one stop light and no cell phone service...grrr...Don't you hate that?).

And he looked completely...normal. The Bible says He "**had no form or majesty that we should look at him, and no beauty that we should desire him**" (Isaiah 53:2). Jesus was no model or movie star. He looked like an average Middle-Eastern man at the time. Dark hair, olive skin, not huge or incredibly muscular by any means.[14]

Think about it this way: Jesus did not stand out AT ALL. He had no formal education. He probably worked with His hands for most of His life as a carpenter.[15] And His bank account was...well, if they'd had bank accounts back then, His would've been empty.[16]

There was NOTHING seemingly "special" about Him. If Jesus walked into your house right now, you might even look down on Him.[17]

It's like what I did at that charity event. The Governor of Ohio was standing in right in front of me, but since he didn't look special, I figured he wasn't special. And I was totally wrong.

Jesus looked like just an average guy. But He was an average guy who was about to change the world.

STAGE THREE: THE SACRIFICE

God began His mission to heal His broken world as a normal-looking guy, walking the dusty roads of Israel.[18] With His miracles He healed broken bodies.[19] With His teaching He healed broken minds and relationships.[20]

Thousands flocked to get a glimpse of this man named Jesus[21] who claimed to have come from Heaven to change the world.[22]

But to accomplish His mission, He needed to go beyond just living among us. In order to fix the brokenness of this world once and for all, Jesus had to truly share in our brokenness. So He did.

> **And being found in human form, he humbled himself by becoming obedient to the point of death, even death on a cross.**

God died.

As a human, Jesus experienced **death**. And this wasn't just any death. It was **death on a cross**.

In order to fix the brokenness of this world once and for all, Jesus had to truly share in our brokenness.

"Okay...so what's the big deal, Joel? It's a cross. My mom wears one on a necklace."

Well, it is a big deal.

Back then...the **cross** signified the most horrible death you could die. It was the worst form of death that people had imagined up to that point. Let me give you just a small peek at a typical crucifixion...

- ***The Beating:*** Before being crucified, the victim was often beaten. Not just with sticks or fists. But also with a whip. A whip with multiple leather strands, each studded with bits of metal and bone. The whip would come down repeatedly, lashing the skin into shreds and taking chunks of flesh with it.[23]
- ***The Nails:*** After being whipped, the victim was marched to the place of execution where he was laid on the beams of the **cross**. Metal spikes were driven into his feet and hands to hold him. Then the **cross** was lifted upright, the victim hanging from its beams.[24]
- ***The Embarrassment:*** Death on a **cross** was humiliating. People would stand at the foot of the **cross** to taunt and make fun of the person hanging there.[25] "Respectable"

people wouldn't even talk about a **cross**,[26] much less do something to get themselves hung on one. It was a death reserved for the lowest of the low. Someone being crucified was considered an outcast and cursed by God.[27]

- ***The End:*** On the **cross**, the victim would have to lift himself up to breathe, but his injuries and extreme fatigue meant doing so would become more and more difficult. Dehydrated and passing in and out of consciousness, sometimes for days, the victim would slowly and painfully suffocate.[28]

Obviously, the **cross** was a horrific way to die. In fact, crucifixion is where we get the word *excruciating*, meaning "intense suffering."[29]

And yet...

The REAL God stepped out of heaven and became a man... for the purpose of dying on a **cross**. It was His plan the entire time. He chose that death on purpose.

On the **cross** God lowered Himself to the very lowest point in human experience. He couldn't get any lower. It couldn't get any darker.

STAGE FOUR: THE VICTORY

But in that moment of darkness...something amazing happened.

Jesus UNdid the greatest evil in all the world; He reversed the power of death.[30]

After dying on the cross, Jesus' body was buried in a tomb.[31] His friends and followers all thought it was the end.[32] But it wasn't.

Three days later, Jesus completed His mission. Three days later, Jesus rose from the dead.[33] Literally. He was 100% dead.[34]

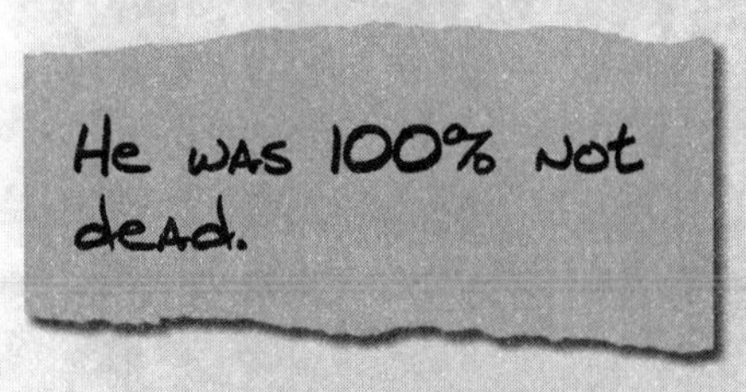

But then, all of a sudden, He was alive.

He was seen eating.[35] He was seen drinking.[36] People touched Him.[37] People talked to Him.[38] Hundreds of people saw Him.[39]

He was 100% not dead.[40]

> **Therefore God has highly exalted him**

Having accomplished his mission by beating death, He returned to His throne in Heaven,[41] raised up (**exalted**) to the highest place.[42]

STAGE FIVE: THE GLORY

"All right, Joel, let me get this straight...so Jesus is God. He came to Earth as a man. He died on a cross. And then He rose from the dead. So what?"

What that means is that Jesus is the REAL God whom we should be worshipping.

Read the last section of this passage:

> **Therefore God has...bestowed on him the name that is above every name, so that at the name of Jesus every knee should bow, in heaven and on earth and under the earth, and every tongue confess that Jesus Christ is Lord, to the glory of God the Father.**

One day, everyone will **bow** before Jesus. One day everyone will acknowledge (**confess**) that He is the True King (**Lord**). One day, **every** being in the universe is going to fall on their faces before King Jesus.

Obviously, it hasn't happened yet. But the day described here... it's coming. Right now He is on His throne, patiently waiting. But He will be recognized for who He really is. It is going to happen.

It's a promise.[43]

THE TRUTH

So here we are in this hotel without windows (see Lie #1). We're looking for answers to the BIG Stuff in the Bible, our OUTSIDE Source, that note slipped under the door (see Lie #2).

But what if...you are sitting in that hotel lobby, thinking about the One who designed, built and owns the hotel...when all of a sudden, IT happens.

You hear a metal latch, and the door swings open. And in walks...a person...in the flesh...from the OUTSIDE! And it's the Owner, Himself![44]

THAT is what Jesus did for us.

And that's why no "Build-A-God" that we can create could possibly match the REAL God we see in Jesus.

He's not "whatever we want Him to be." He isn't a push-over or some magic genie in the sky. He's not like the FAKE gods we create for ourselves: our friends, our image, our experiences, our accomplishments or our desires (see Lie #3). The REAL God, the God of the Bible, did what no FAKE god has ever done.

He came on a mission. He stepped down from His throne to walk on this earth and defeat death. And then He stepped back up into heaven and took His rightful place again.

He came to Earth to heal our broken world. And He still offers healing to all who worship Him.[15]

That is the God of the Bible, the REAL God, and His name is Jesus.

And that leaves us only one possible question...how can I start worshipping this Jesus?

Well, that leads us right to Lie #5...

MAKING IT PERSONAL

1. Was there a time when you (or someone you know) made a mistake similar to Joel's mistake with the governor? What happened?

____

____

____

2. Had you ever thought about Batman and Jesus having a similar mission? What do you think about that comparison?

____

____

____

3. Why is it hard for people to believe that Jesus is the REAL God? Why is that an important truth to understand about Jesus' identity?

____

____

____

4. Jesus died on a cross. What, if anything, in the description of crucifixion grabbed your attention?

____

____

____

5. **Do you have difficulty believing the Bible passage from this chapter when it says that everyone will one day bow before Jesus? Why or why not?**

____

____

____

6. **What "Build-a-Bear" views of God do people you know have that don't fit with what the Bible says? How does the passage in this chapter differ from their ideas about Jesus, the REAL God?**

____

____

____

NOTES

1 Of course, I don't really believe in "luck." By "I think I just got lucky," I mean that things worked out to favor me in a way that I didn't expect, given the circumstances.

2 John 1:1 - *In the beginning was the Word, and the Word was with God, and the Word was God.* Also John 1:14 - *And the Word became flesh and dwelt among us, and we have seen his glory, glory as of the only Son from the Father, full of grace and truth.*

3 John 1:18 - *No one has ever seen God; the only God, who is at the Father's side, he has made him known.* Also John 14:9 - *Jesus said to him, "Have I been with you so long, and you still do not know me, Philip? Whoever has seen me has seen the Father. How can you say, 'Show us the Father'?*

4 J. F. Walvoord, R. B. Zuck, & Dallas Theological Seminary. *The Bible Knowledge Commentary : An Exposition of the Scriptures* (Wheaton, IL: Victor, 1983) n.p. Also, Henry Bettenson, and Chris Maunder, eds. *Documents of the Christian Church.* New ed. (Oxford: Oxford, 1999) 28. Walvoord stresses the term "essence" here, while Bettenson notes that the Nicene Creed uses the term "substance."

5 Colossians 1:16 - *For by him all things were created, in heaven and on earth, visible and invisible, whether thrones or dominions or rulers or authorities—all things were created through him and for him.*

6 Psalm 89:11 - *The heavens are yours; the earth also is yours; the world and all that is in it, you have founded them.*

7 Psalm 103:19 - *The LORD has established his throne in the heavens, and his kingdom rules over all.*

8 Revelation 19:16 - *On his robe and on his thigh he has a name written, King of kings and Lord of lords.*

9 2 Corinthians 8:9 - *For you know the grace of our Lord Jesus Christ, that though he was rich, yet for your sake he became poor, so that you by his poverty might become rich.*

10 Bettenson, 65.

11 Luke 2:7 - *And she gave birth to her firstborn son and wrapped him in swaddling cloths and laid him in a manger, because there was no place for them in the inn.*

[12] Matthew 13:55 - *Is not this the carpenter's son? Is not his mother called Mary? And are not his brothers James and Joseph and Simon and Judas?*

[13] Micah 5:2 - *But you, O Bethlehem Ephrathah, who are too little to be among the clans of Judah, from you shall come forth for me one who is to be ruler in Israel, whose coming forth is from of old, from ancient days.* Also John 7:42 - *Has not the Scripture said that the Christ comes from the offspring of David, and comes from Bethlehem, the village where David was?*

[14] I'm not saying Jesus probably didn't have good muscle tone. By "incredibly muscular," I mean big and built to an extent that it would really make him stand out, which would be contrary to Isaiah 53:2 - *For he grew up before him like a young plant, and like a root out of dry ground; he had no form or majesty that we should look at him, and no beauty that we should desire him.*

[15] Mark 6:3 - *Is not this the carpenter, the son of Mary and brother of James and Joses and Judas and Simon? And are not his sisters here with us?" And they took offense at him.*

[16] Matthew 8:20 - *And Jesus said to him, "Foxes have holes, and birds of the air have nests, but the Son of Man has nowhere to lay his head."*

[17] John 1:45–46 - *Philip found Nathanael and said to him, "We have found him of whom Moses in the Law and also the prophets wrote, Jesus of Nazareth, the son of Joseph." Nathanael said to him, "Can anything good come out of Nazareth?" Philip said to him, "Come and see."*

[18] John 6:42 - *They said, "Is not this Jesus, the son of Joseph, whose father and mother we know? How does he now say, 'I have come down from heaven'?"*

[19] Matthew 9:35 - *And Jesus went throughout all the cities and villages, teaching in their synagogues and proclaiming the gospel of the kingdom and healing every disease and every affliction.*

[20] See "The Sermon on the Mount" in Matthew, chapters 5-7. Also, Matthew 7:28–29 - *And when Jesus finished these sayings, the crowds were astonished at his teaching, for he was teaching them as one who had authority, and not as their scribes.*

[21] Matthew 8:1 - *When he came down from the mountain, great crowds followed him.*

[22] John 6:29–33 - *Jesus answered them, "This is the work of God, that you believe in him whom he has sent." So they said to him, "Then what sign do*

you do, that we may see and believe you? What work do you perform? Our fathers ate the manna in the wilderness; as it is written, 'He gave them bread from heaven to eat.'" Jesus then said to them, "Truly, truly, I say to you, it was not Moses who gave you the bread from heaven, but my Father gives you the true bread from heaven. For the bread of God is he who comes down from heaven and gives life to the world."

[23] McDowell, *The Best*, 222.

[24] McDowell, *The Best*, 223.

[25] Mark 15:29–30 - *And those who passed by derided him, wagging their heads and saying, "Aha! You who would destroy the temple and rebuild it in three days, save yourself, and come down from the cross!"* Also, Luke 23:36 - *The soldiers also mocked him, coming up and offering him sour wine.*

[26] Brent Kercheville. "Mark 15:21-41, The Crucifixion of Jesus." West Palm Beach Church of Christ, 2011. Web. 20 July 2011. In a transcript of this sermon, Kercheville quotes the Roman historian, Cicero, as saying, "Let the very mention of the cross be far removed not only from a Roman citizen's body, but from his mind, his eyes, his ears."

[27] Galatians 3:13 - *Christ redeemed us from the curse of the law by becoming a curse for us—for it is written, "Cursed is everyone who is hanged on a tree."*

[28] McDowell, *The Best*, 224.

[29] "Excruciate." *Online Etymological Dictionary*. 2010. Web. 20 July 2011.

[30] Hebrews 2:14 - *Since therefore the children share in flesh and blood, he [Jesus] himself likewise partook of the same things, that through death he might destroy the one who has the power of death, that is, the devil,*

[31] John 19:38–41 - *After these things Joseph of Arimathea, who was a disciple of Jesus, but secretly for fear of the Jews, asked Pilate that he might take away the body of Jesus, and Pilate gave him permission. So he came and took away his body. Nicodemus also, who earlier had come to Jesus by night, came bringing a mixture of myrrh and aloes, about seventy-five pounds in weight. So they took the body of Jesus and bound it in linen cloths with the spices, as is the burial custom of the Jews. Now in the place where he was crucified there was a garden, and in the garden a new tomb in which no one had yet been laid.*

[32] Luke 24:21 - *But we had hoped that he was the one to redeem Israel. Yes, and besides all this, it is now the third day since these things happened.*

[33] Luke 24:46 - *and said to them, "Thus it is written, that the Christ should suffer and on the third day rise from the dead,*

[34] John 19:30–33 - *When Jesus had received the sour wine, he said, "It is finished," and he bowed his head and gave up his spirit. Since it was the day of Preparation, and so that the bodies would not remain on the cross on the Sabbath (for that Sabbath was a high day), the Jews asked Pilate that their legs might be broken and that they might be taken away. So the soldiers came and broke the legs of the first, and of the other who had been crucified with him. But when they came to Jesus and saw that he was already dead, they did not break his legs.* See also, William Lane Craig. *Reasonable Faith: Christian Faith and Apologetics* (Wheaton, IL: Crossway, 1994) 279. Some people claim that Jesus did not die on the cross. This is called the "Swoon Theory" or the "Apparent Death Theory." William Lane Craig does a great job of explaining why this theory is silly.

[35] Luke 24:41–43 - *And while they still disbelieved for joy and were marveling, he said to them, "Have you anything here to eat?" They gave him a piece of broiled fish, and he took it and ate before them.*

[36] Acts 10:41 - *not to all the people but to us who had been chosen by God as witnesses, who ate and drank with him after he rose from the dead.*

[37] John 20:27 - *Then he said to Thomas, "Put your finger here, and see my hands; and put out your hand, and place it in my side. Do not disbelieve, but believe."*

[38] John 21:15 - *When they had finished breakfast, Jesus said to Simon Peter, "Simon, son of John, do you love me more than these?" He said to him, "Yes, Lord; you know that I love you." He said to him, "Feed my lambs."*

[39] 1 *Corinthians 15:4–6 - that he was buried, that he was raised on the third day in accordance with the Scriptures, and that he appeared to Cephas, then to the twelve. Then he appeared to more than five hundred brothers at one time, most of whom are still alive, though some have fallen asleep.*

[40] The evidence for the resurrection of Jesus is extensive. There are many resources where you can read about the evidence. I recommend *The Case for Christ* by Lee Strobel for light readers and *Reasonable Faith* by William Lane Craig for people who think they're smart.

[41] Hebrews 12:2 - *looking to Jesus, the founder and perfecter of our faith, who for the joy that was set before him endured the cross, despising the shame, and is seated at the right hand of the throne of God.*

[42] Hebrews 1:3 - *He is the radiance of the glory of God and the exact imprint of his nature, and he upholds the universe by the word of his power. After making purification for sins, he sat down at the right hand of the Majesty on high,*

[43] Matthew 25:31–32 - *When the Son of Man comes in his glory, and all the angels with him, then he will sit on his glorious throne. Before him will be gathered all the nations, and he will separate people one from another as a shepherd separates the sheep from the goats.*

[44] One might say the analogy is breaking down here because, as Chapter 3 explains, the door is locked from the inside. So the owner shouldn't be able to unlock the door. Well, the owner is God, and trust me, He wouldn't have trouble picking the lock.

[45] Isaiah 53:5 - *But he was wounded for our transgressions; he was crushed for our iniquities; upon him was the chastisement that brought us peace, and with his stripes we are healed.* Also, 1 Peter 2:24 - *He himself bore our sins in his body on the tree, that we might die to sin and live to righteousness. By his wounds you have been healed.*

WARNING

This chapter will offend you.

If you're getting tired of my tell-it-like-it-is tone, you should know...it's about to get worse. Much worse. And maybe you should just put the book down right now.

I hope you keep reading because this is actually the most important chapter of the book. I could have left this part out to spare your feelings, but this is stuff you REALLY need to know.

The lie I am about to address has most likely been driven deep into your brain. You hear it so often from so many different people that you will probably think that I'm the one who has it wrong. You might not even understand what I am trying to say. Because of that, I am going to have to hit hard. I'm going to have to make my words like a jack hammer in order to penetrate your brain and knock the Lie loose.

It will probably be painful. You may think that I am cold and don't have a heart. You might even get angry.

But I hope you will push through and hear me out.

You have been warned.

LIE #5:

"YOU'RE A WINNER."

A Lesson From The Biggest Loser

Do you watch *The Biggest Loser*? I'll admit it...I do. It's hard for me to admit that because...while I'm watching it, half of me is holding back vomit.

"Okay, Joel. That's a bit dramatic, don't you think?"

No, I don't, and I'll tell you why.

Most people find the show totally inspiring. They say, "It's just so awesome to watch these contestants working so hard for such an incredible goal. They really push themselves to become the best they can be. It's just so impressive."

Hmm...I guess.

I see it a little differently. I think that show is a bunch of crap. It's nothing more than one big advertisement for Lie #5. It makes me want to puke.

I see it a little differently. I think that show is a bunch of crap.

Every week the contestants look at the camera, tears rolling down their faces, and sob, "For the first time in my life...I really love myself."

The trainers, the counseling sessions, everything in the show tells them (and us) that their real problem, the reason they are overweight, is that they have lived for everyone BUT themselves. And now, finally, it's time to change all that.

"Love yourself. Do it for yourself. You are worth it. You are a winner...so treat yourself that way."

"NO. NO. NO. You aren't! AAAAAHH!!" I scream at the TV.

AN EVERYDAY LIE

"I don't get it, Joel. What's your problem with the show?"

It's not the show, exactly. My problem is Lie #5. We hear it everywhere. Your teachers, your friends, maybe even your parents. They all say that you need to love yourself more.

"You just need more self-confidence," we're told. "Accept yourself for who you are."

So, these days, everyone gets a ribbon just for participating. Like the people on *The Biggest Loser,* we're supposed to feel good about ourselves. We get patted on the back and told that we are winners.

But it's a lie. And frankly...it makes me want to throw up (Have I mentioned that yet?).

Now, don't get me wrong. I think what they are doing is great. I am all about making and keeping commitments. (Did you read the book I wrote about commitments?) I am also all about achievement and competition, especially when it drives us to be the best we can be. Oh, and I'm all about being healthy, too. Though I could probably stand to lose a few pounds myself...okay...maybe 50.

But here's the thing...none of us are winners. We are all losers.

"So you're saying the people on Biggest Loser...are losers?"

Yes, I am. But I'm NOT talking about their weight. Seriously, this whole rant has NOTHING to do with their weight.

I am talking about the fact that they, like all of us, love themselves TOO MUCH (not too little). This is the fundamental problem for every human being on this earth. We don't need more self confidence...we need to think less of ourselves!

And when contestants on the *Biggest Loser* say things like, "For the first time in my life, I am living for myself..." this becomes all too obvious.

I'm serious. Think about it. Were the contestants really "living for" other people before they went on the show? Um...I don't know...when was the last time you ate a couple extra pieces of pizza for someone else?

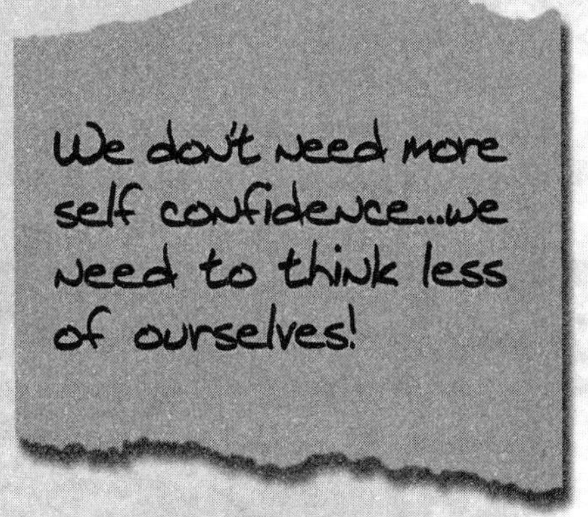

No, they are overweight because they wouldn't deny *themselves* the pleasure of food. Every poor choice they made that resulted in obesity was NOT because they didn't love themselves. It was precisely because they DID love themselves...too much!

"Wow, Joel. Clearly you don't understand that obesity is a much more complex problem."

Hey, I don't deny that it's complex. I know there are genetic issues, environmental issues, educational issues, emotional issues and addiction issues. But I'm talking about something deeper than those things. At the foundational level it all really comes down to one issue: worship...self-worship (see Lie #3).

You see, we have all betrayed the REAL God to worship ourselves. And self-worship shows up in our lives in countless ways, whether it's over-spending, over-sleeping, over-TV watching, or over-eating. It could even be over-exercising or under-eating or a million other things.

The point is that we already love ourselves more than we love anyone or anything on this earth.

And that makes us all losers. You. Me. Everybody. The honest truth is...we suck.

"Come on, Joel. I'm a nice person. Ease up a bit, will ya?"

Um...no. I can't ease up. You might think you are a good person, but...you're not. You might think that you are good enough, but...you're not.

It's time someone looked you in the eye and told you the truth.

You suck. And you need to deal with that fact.[1]

APPROACHING THE JUDGE

Okay, so why did I feel the need to insult you like that?

Actually, I'm trying to protect you from a disaster. Let me explain.

We just finished Lie #4 asking the question, "How can I start worshipping Jesus?" And you need to know that the first step in approaching Jesus is coming to the realization that you have failed.[2]

We are not naturally good people.[3] We haven't done anything to win God's approval.[4] And we don't deserve to be accepted by God.[5]

This is different than what you'll hear from just about every other religion in the world. Most people will say that if you are "good enough," God will accept you.

But the Bible says that if we think for a minute that there is ANYTHING "good" in us that can earn God's approval, we are fooling ourselves and setting ourselves up for a catastrophe.[6]

Do you remember William Hung? He was one of the most famously bad contestants on *American Idol* back in the day. He danced (sort of) while (sort of) singing Ricky Martin's *She Bangs* for the judges. He was terrible. And it was totally entertaining (Seriously...YouTube it).[7]

In fact, a lot of the early auditions each season on *American Idol* are just ridiculous. These people swear they can sing ("Everyone says so"). They act like they have something to offer the judges. They actually expect to hear praise. But when they open their mouths...they sound like a cat that just got shot with a BB gun.

It's sad really. They think they're so good. But in reality, they suck. Really, really bad. And we sit in our comfy chairs, shaking our heads in amazement. How could they be so bad and not even know it?

But...we do the same thing. We might think we are good enough to please God. But we aren't. We might think we have something to offer God. But we don't. We might think that we can earn God's approval. But we can't.

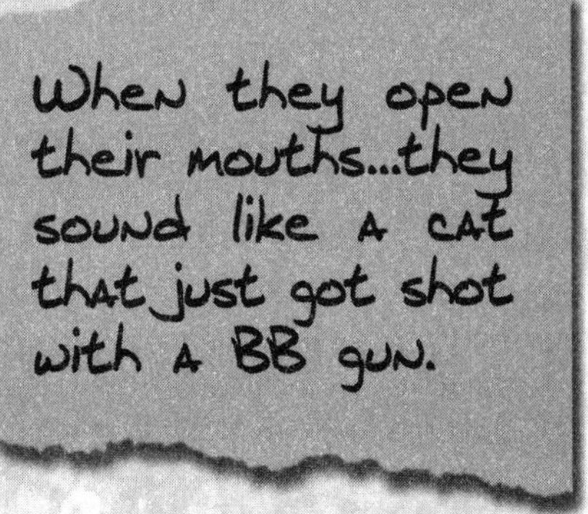

And if we think we can do ANYTHING that will "impress" God, we look as ridiculous as William Hung.

You NEED to understand this.

Because when we approach God, we don't audition for the judges of *American Idol.* We stand before the Judge of the Universe.[8] And by His standards, we are anything but winners.

Check it out:

> **For while we were still weak, at the right time Christ died for the ungodly. For one will scarcely die for a righteous person though perhaps for a good person one would dare even to die but God shows his love for us in that while we were still sinners, Christ died for us. Since, therefore, we have now been justified by his blood, much more shall we be saved by him from the wrath of God. For if while we were enemies we were reconciled to God by the death of his Son, much more, now that we are reconciled, shall we be saved by his life. More than that, we also rejoice in God through our Lord Jesus Christ, through whom we have now received reconciliation. (Romans 5:6–11)**

Again, that's a big chunk of words. But the message is pretty simple.

Let's break it down.

THE TRIAL

Our trial was over before it ever started.

In God's eyes, this is a cut-and-dry case. God, the Judge, is sitting on his bench looking at the worst of the worst. This criminal is guilty. It's not a matter of whether he's done enough good to get by. There's nothing good on his record. Not one thing.[9]

We can blame his environment or his family or his circumstances. But every choice he's ever made has been wrong. Everything he's ever done has been bad. The best he's got to offer is as worthless as last week's garbage.[10]

Sound harsh? It is. But it's precisely how the Bible describes each of us. Check it out:

> **For while we were still weak, at the right time Christ died for the ungodly.**

When God looks at us, He sees **weak**ness. People without strength. People who are sick, impotent, and feeble. Who can't do anything for themselves. It's not a pretty picture.

And it gets worse. We are also **ungodly**. We have no reverence for God. It's not that we aren't religious...no we're worse than that. We actively oppose God.

We are so far down the ladder that we have absolutely no hope at all. And to make sure we don't miss how beyond pathetic our situation is, the Bible continues...

> **For one will scarcely die for a righteous person though perhaps for a good person one would dare even to die**

It's a simple question, really: "Who would you die to save?"

A **good person**? The really good ones, the Mother Theresa types. Would you die for Mother Theresa? Well, we'd like to think so. If we had to give up our life to save someone else, we'd most likely want to save someone who's doing the really, really good stuff.

Okay, well, how about a **righteous** person? This guy isn't going to win sainthood, but he's basically nice. He gives to charity. He does some good stuff. He's your normal, average "nice guy."

Would you die for that guy? Maybe. It's less likely than Mother Theresa...but it could still happen.

Okay, so now we get to the real issue. Would you die to save a mass murderer? The guy who raped your sister? A child molester? Hitler? Would you have died to save Osama bin Laden?

"Absolutely not, Joel. That's crazy. Those guys deserve to pay."

And that's the point. We would never die for a real scumbag. We'd never give our lives for a true criminal.

But in God's eyes, WE are ALL real scumbags...true criminals. Check it out:

we were still sinners

See, in God's courtroom, we're **sinners**. We do bad things, think bad things, have bad attitudes, and generally have nothing in us that could be considered "**righteous**" or "**good**."

That's what God saw when He looked at us. On our own, that's where every person on this planet is in comparison to God.

And the Bible is pretty clear about where we stand: "**None is righteous, no, not one; no one understands; no one seeks for God. All have turned aside; together they have become worthless; no one does good, not even one.**" **(Romans 3:10-12)**

In other words, God's wrath is legitimate. We are totally guilty of everything we're being accused of. We betrayed God. And our betrayal has a price...a price that must be paid.

And what is the price? Well, we said we didn't want God, so we will get our wish. Our punishment is total and eternal separation from God and His love.[11] No more of the good things from God that we enjoy on this earth.[12] We will be banished forever to a place of torment and punishment. We will be separated from all that is good forever...in Hell.[13]

That is our sentence. That is the Court's decision. Case closed.[14]

A GLIMMER OF HOPE

Except...for one thing. Or, more accurately, one Person.

See, the REAL God is not *only* a just and wrathful Judge. He is also a loving Father. He is a Father who wants a relationship with His created children (us).[15]

But there's a problem.

If God is a just Judge... and if we are guilty **sinners**...then we deserve a just sentence. We deserve God's wrath. There must be punishment for our betrayal, or God is unjust.

See, the REAL God is not only a just and wrathful Judge. He is also a loving Father.

So how can God be perfectly just AND not condemn guilty people?

Answer: Jesus.

Jesus stepped in as our SINLESS Substitute.

Look at our verses again.

> **at the right time Christ died (for) the ungodly... God shows his love for us in that while we were still sinners, Christ died (for) us**

We were **sinners**. Jesus was sinless.

We were evil. Jesus was righteous.

We deserved death. Jesus deserved life.

But He stood in our place and died our death. He endured the wrath of God so we don't have to.

Jesus died **for** us.

THE GREAT EXCHANGE[16]

The Bible describes it this way:

> **We have now been justified by his blood**

Now don't freak out. The word **justify** is actually a really simple concept. It's a legal term which basically means that the Judge declares you righteous.

Think about it like this...

We are back in God's courtroom. We are guilty. There's no appeal, no chance of a mistrial, no getting off on a technicality. The gavel is about to fall.

But then, at the last second, a voice comes from the back of the courtroom. "I will take his place."

It's Jesus, the Judge's own Son. Everyone in the place knows He isn't guilty of your crimes. But He willingly steps beside you, accepts your sentence and takes your place in custody. He substitutes Himself for you. And as Jesus is being led away in your handcuffs to the place of execution, the Judge says to you, "I find you not guilty. You have been **justified**. You are free to go."

That's what Jesus did for us. Jesus, the King of heaven, took on Himself our sin, our filth, our evil, when He spilled His **blood** on that cross. He took our punishment and paid our debt as our SINLESS Substitute.[17]

And because He did, God no longer sees us as **weak** and **ungodly** and **sinful**. He calls us righteous. The Judge declares that we are "right with God."

> He took our punishment and paid our debt as our SINLESS Substitute.

But being **justified** isn't the end. Just like a "guilty" verdict would have huge consequences, our "not guilty" verdict results in huge rewards. The passage mentions two:

> **Since, therefore, we have now been justified by his blood, much more shall we be saved by him from the wrath of God...we also rejoice in God through our Lord Jesus Christ, through whom we have now received reconciliation.**

1. We get **reconciliation.**

It's a big word, but it's a simple concept.

We ran away from home. We were God's enemies.[18] But now, we are invited back into a relationship with God. And He welcomes us with open arms.[19]

The Judge now invites us to a "Welcome Home" party in His chambers. We, the creation, are finally reunited (**reconciled**) with our Creator.[20]

2. We will be **saved.**

"Saved from what?"

Exactly what the passage says. We will be **saved** from the **wrath of God**.

So far we've been talking about an imaginary courtroom scene. BUT, according to the Bible, there is a real day of judgment coming.[21]

After this life, we will all stand in front of our Creator to be judged for our actions. And we will be on trial for our eternal lives.[22]

We will have to answer for betraying the REAL God and worshipping FAKE gods. And the Bible says that on THAT day, God will justly pour out His **wrath** on mankind by sending people to an eternal Hell...infinite punishment for dishonoring an infinitely honorable God.[23]

But on THAT day we will be **saved** from the punishment we deserve because of what Jesus did on the cross.[24]

We can be **reconciled** to God now and **saved** from the wrath of God in the future. All because of Jesus, our SINLESS Substitute who died **for** us.

THE JUDGE'S CHAMBERS

So what's left? A choice. Your choice.

Yes, Jesus made all of this amazing stuff possible. But it won't do you any good unless you receive it.

Go back to our little courtroom scene above...because I left out a really important moment in the story. You're waiting for your sentence. Jesus has volunteered to take your place. And the Judge turns to you.

"Do you accept?" He asks you.

You have a choice. A simple "yes" means you get the "not guilty" verdict, the "Welcome Home' party, and the escape from future punishment. A "no" leaves you under the sentence we each deserve. And it's totally up to you.

The Bible describes that choice this way: "**Through him we have also obtained access by faith into this grace in which we stand.**" (**Romans 5:2**)

"What does that mean?"

Well, let's start with **grace**. **Grace** is a gift. A gift that is UNDESERVED and UNEARNED.[25] Like if you're walking down the street, and out of nowhere someone hands you a $100 bill. It's undeserved and unearned. That's **grace**.

We don't deserve God's love. We haven't earned God's forgiveness. But God offers them to us anyway. **Grace** is the invitation to enter the Judge's chambers, having been forgiven your crimes, not because you deserve it...but just because He wants to give it to you.

And **faith**? Basically, **faith** is trust.

Faith means trusting God when He says you can't earn His approval.

Faith means trusting Jesus to earn God's approval for you.

Faith means trusting Jesus with your life...with your forever.

In other words, when the Judge asks if you accept... you say "yes" by placing your **faith** (trust) in Jesus. And **faith** gives you **access** to God's **grace**.

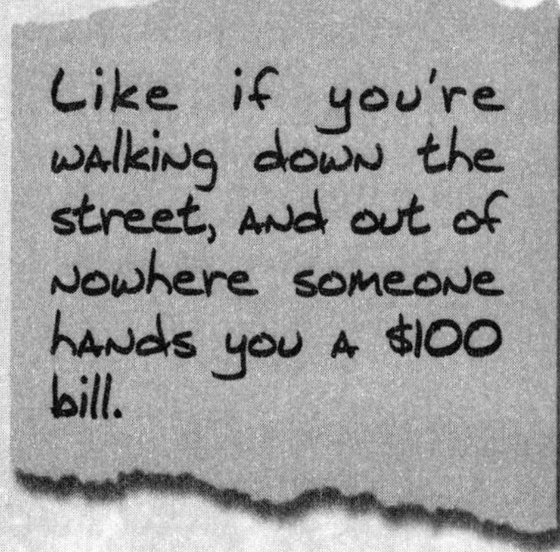

"OK... but what does faith in Jesus really look like?"

Well, **faith** itself doesn't really "look" like anything because it's invisible. It's internal.[26]

But real, internal **faith** might be best described as a "turn." It's turning from one thing to another.[27]

1. ***Turning from Self*** - You must abandon all your attempts to impress God or earn His love. Admit that you have betrayed the REAL God to worship FAKE gods, especially the god of self. Make the conscious decision in your heart and mind to turn away from living for yourself and your other FAKE gods as best you know how.

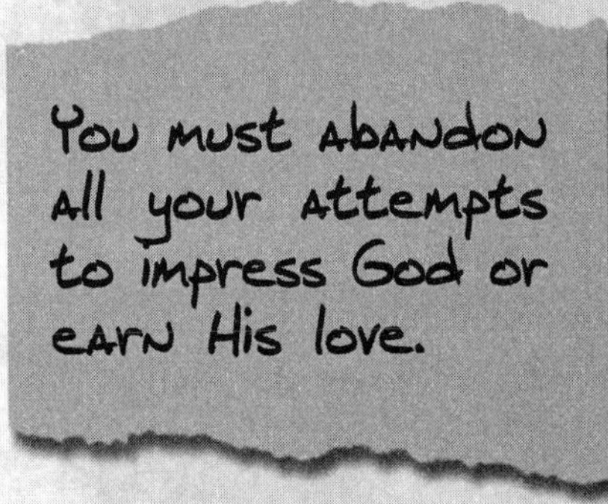

2. ***Turning to Jesus*** - You must ask Jesus to forgive you. Ask Him to rescue you from the penalty of your rebellion against God. Ask Him to **reconcile** you to a real relationship with God. Believe in Jesus, His death on the cross, and His resurrection from the dead. Trust Him to **save** you.

Some people I know have made their turn of **faith** this way. They prayed:

> *Dear Jesus,*
>
> *Thank you for dying in my place. I admit that I have failed to live for you. Please forgive my rebellion and save me from the consequences. I am choosing to turn from myself and to you. I believe in you, and I trust you to accept me not based on anything I have done, but because of what you have done for me.*[28]

A real turn of **faith** "looks" kind of like that.

THE TRUTH

So the cold, hard truth might not be what you want to hear. We all suck. We are not winners. And we have no hope of earning God's approval.

Our relationship with God is broken. It needs to be healed.

And Jesus died to do just that. He paid the penalty for all that we have done wrong. He was our SINLESS Substitute. And when we have trust (**faith**) in Jesus, we have access to the gift (**grace**) that God provided for us when Jesus died on that cross.

No other way will get us connected (**reconciled**) to God. No other way will rescue (**save**) us from future judgment. We only get **access** to what God offers by **faith**.

And you know what? That's amazing! The REAL God of the Universe loves us so much that He sacrificed Himself to rescue us. And He offers us this gift completely free of charge.

We don't earn it. We don't pay for it. We don't work for it. God's gift is free.

This is the greatest news in all the world!

So...what do you think? Are you buying any of this? Have you made the turn of **faith**?

Maybe you totally agree with everything you've read. Maybe you still think I am crazy or on crack. Maybe you're wondering, *"So...faith in Jesus is all we need? That's it? That's the end?"*

Well, yes and no. Is it all we need to receive God's forgiveness?...yes. But is it the end?...not really.

Actually, it's just the beginning. On to Lie #6...

MAKING IT PERSONAL

1. Do you think Joel's argument that "we all suck" because of our self-worship is too harsh? Not harsh enough? Do you think he is right? Why or why not?

2. What are some ways that people try to "earn" God's approval? According to the Bible passage in this chapter, why won't they work?

3. What is your reaction to the idea in the Bible that God is our Judge? Is that image of God hard for you to accept? Why or why not?

4. The Bible says God is both wrathful Judge and loving Father. But many people tend to emphasize one side or the other. Why do you think people have trouble emphasizing both?

5. **Jesus is our SINLESS Substitute. Can you describe the exchange that happened when He took our place? What was ours that He took? What of His did we get? What is your response to that truth?**

____

____

____

6. **To come to God by faith is a decision to turn from self to Jesus. Have you ever made a "turn of faith" like the one described in the chapter?**

____

____

____

NOTES

1 Some may question my usage of the word "suck" to describe our idolatrous state because it is very negative and has a sexual connotation. The Bible uses the word "whore" 78 times to describe idolatrous people. I don't think "suck" is any more negative or sexual. If anything, it might be a little weak.

2 James 4:9–10 - *Be wretched and mourn and weep. Let your laughter be turned to mourning and your joy to gloom. Humble yourselves before the Lord, and he will exalt you.*

3 Psalm 51:5 - *Behold, I was brought forth in iniquity, and in sin did my mother conceive me.* Also, Jeremiah 17:9 - *The heart is deceitful above all things, and desperately sick; who can understand it?*

4 Isaiah 64:6 - *We have all become like one who is unclean, and all our righteous deeds are like a polluted garment. We all fade like a leaf, and our iniquities, like the wind, take us away.*

5 Ephesians 2:3 - *among whom we all once lived in the passions of our flesh, carrying out the desires of the body and the mind, and were by nature children of wrath, like the rest of mankind.*

6 Luke 18:10–14 - *"Two men went up into the temple to pray, one a Pharisee and the other a tax collector. The Pharisee, standing by himself, prayed thus: 'God, I thank you that I am not like other men, extortioners, unjust, adulterers, or even like this tax collector. I fast twice a week; I give tithes of all that I get.' But the tax collector, standing far off, would not even lift up his eyes to heaven, but beat his breast, saying, 'God, be merciful to me, a sinner!' I tell you, this man went down to his house justified, rather than the other. For everyone who exalts himself will be humbled, but the one who humbles himself will be exalted."*

7 Check out William Hung's audition on YouTube: http://www.youtube.com/watch?v=9RrLQUN8UJg

8 Psalm 7:11 - *God is a righteous judge, and a God who feels indignation every day. And, Genesis 18:25 - Far be it from you to do such a thing, to put the righteous to death with the wicked, so that the righteous fare as the wicked! Far be that from you! Shall not the Judge of all the earth do what is just?"*

9 Romans 3:12 - *All have turned aside; together they have become worthless; no one does good, not even one.*

10 Isaiah 64:6 - *We have all become like one who is unclean, and all our righteous deeds are like a polluted garment. We all fade like a leaf, and our iniquities, like the wind, take us away.*

[11] 2 Thessalonians 1:9 - *They will suffer the punishment of eternal destruction, away from the presence of the Lord and from the glory of his might,*

[12] Matthew 5:45 - *so that you may be sons of your Father who is in heaven. For he makes his sun rise on the evil and on the good, and sends rain on the just and on the unjust.*

[13] Matthew 25:46 - *And these will go away into eternal punishment, but the righteous into eternal life.*

[14] John 3:17–18 - *For God did not send his Son into the world to condemn the world, but in order that the world might be saved through him. Whoever believes in him is not condemned, but whoever does not believe is condemned already, because he has not believed in the name of the only Son of God.*

[15] 2 Corinthians 6:18 - *and I will be a father to you, and you shall be sons and daughters to me, says the Lord Almighty.* Also, John 4:23 - *But the hour is coming, and is now here, when the true worshipers will worship the Father in spirit and truth, for the Father is seeking such people to worship him.*

[16] Paul Althaus. *Theology of Martin Luther.* (Philadelphia: Fortress, 1966) 213. Martin Luther originated this terminology, although he called it the "wonderful exchange" in his writings.

[17] Romans 3:23–25 - *for all have sinned and fall short of the glory of God, and are justified by his grace as a gift, through the redemption that is in Christ Jesus, whom God put forward as a propitiation by his blood, to be received by faith. This was to show God's righteousness, because in his divine forbearance he had passed over former sins.* Also, 2 Corinthians 5:21 - *For our sake he made him to be sin who knew no sin, so that in him we might become the righteousness of God.*

[18] Colossians 1:21 - *And you, who once were alienated and hostile in mind, doing evil deeds.* Also, Romans 5:10 - *For if while we were enemies we were reconciled to God by the death of his Son, much more, now that we are reconciled, shall we be saved by his life.*

[19] See the parable of the Prodigal son in Luke, chapter 15, where God is portrayed as a loving Father who welcomes home his son who had gone astray. Luke 15:20 - *And he arose and came to his father. But while he was still a long way off, his father saw him and felt compassion, and ran and embraced him and kissed him.*

[20] 2 Corinthians 5:18–19 - *All this is from God, who through Christ reconciled us to himself and gave us the ministry of reconciliation; that is, in Christ God was reconciling the world to himself, not counting their trespasses against them, and entrusting to us the message of reconciliation.* Also,

Colossians 1:21–22 - *And you, who once were alienated and hostile in mind, doing evil deeds, he has now reconciled in his body of flesh by his death, in order to present you holy and blameless and above reproach before him,*

21 Matthew 12:36 - *I tell you, on the day of judgment people will give account for every careless word they speak,*

22 Revelation 20:11–13 - *Then I saw a great white throne and him who was seated on it. From his presence earth and sky fled away, and no place was found for them. And I saw the dead, great and small, standing before the throne, and books were opened. Then another book was opened, which is the book of life. And the dead were judged by what was written in the books, according to what they had done. And the sea gave up the dead who were in it, Death and Hades gave up the dead who were in them, and they were judged, each one of them, according to what they had done.*

23 Revelation 20:14–15 - *Then Death and Hades were thrown into the lake of fire. This is the second death, the lake of fire. And if anyone's name was not found written in the book of life, he was thrown into the lake of fire.*

24 2 Corinthians 5:21 - *For our sake he made him to be sin who knew no sin, so that in him we might become the righteousness of God.*

25 Romans 11:6 - *But if it is by grace, it is no longer on the basis of works; otherwise grace would no longer be grace.* Also, Ephesians 2:8–9 - *For by grace you have been saved through faith. And this is not your own doing; it is the gift of God, not a result of works, so that no one may boast.*

26 The effects of faith are very visible (James 2:18 - *But someone will say, "You have faith and I have works." Show me your faith apart from your works, and I will show you my faith by my works),* but faith itself is invisible.

27 I am using the word "turn" as a synonym of "repent" which the Bible frequently uses. True faith involves repentance, and true repentance involves faith. That is why the two words are sometimes used interchangeably in the Bible when summarizing the gospel (compare Acts 3:19 – *"Repent therefore, and turn again, that your sins may be blotted out,"* with Acts 16:31 - *And they said, "Believe in the Lord Jesus, and you will be saved, you and your household."*). This is why I am using the concept of a "turn of faith."

28 Timothy Keller. *The Reason for God: Belief in an Age of Skepticism* (New York: Riverhead, 2008) 245. The prayer I give here was modeled after the prayer that Keller uses in his book.

LIE #6:

"ALL PEOPLE ARE THE SAME."

A Lesson From A Couple Babies

I stumbled across the room in the dark, frantically feeling around for my book bag. The baby's crying got louder. Finally, I gave in and turned on the light. There it was!

I grabbed my bag, feeling in the front pocket for the key. "Thank Goodness!" I thought, dropping the bag as I lunged back over all the stuff on the floor to pick up my baby. I jammed the plastic key into its back and the crying stopped. Instant relief.

Unfortunately, though, that wasn't enough. Holding the baby with one hand, I had to keep pressure on the key with my other hand. It was an awkward position, especially at 3 a.m., but it was better than listening to the mechanical crying sound of my computerized baby. After several minutes, I finally was able to climb back into my bunk bed and close my eyes.

"Wow," I thought, "Mrs. Stevenson was right. This is annoying!"

Mrs. Stevenson was my 8th grade health teacher. And I was right in the middle of Sex Ed. For two weeks, every student had to carry around an electronic baby which recorded whether it was dropped, or starved, or left to cry too long. It was supposed to scare us about the responsibilities and reality of teen pregnancy.

Trust me...it worked. But then...

12 years later:

It was the middle of the night, and my baby was crying...again.

But this time, there was no book bag and no key. This was my son. I rolled out of bed and headed down the hallway to the nursery.

There he was, totally helpless, a tiny fuzzy head sticking out of his blue fuzzy blankets. He was crying, loudly. His eyes were shut, and his mouth was wide open. His face was all red. And he stunk, badly.

I picked him up and quickly started to deal with the stench. Man, this kid could poop! Finally, I managed to get his diaper changed and started gently bouncing him on my knee.

The crying stopped, no plastic key needed.

He opened his eyes and smiled up at me. Then he opened his mouth and threw up all over my chest. "Nice," I thought, laughing at how quickly his emotions had changed, and how dirty and stinky this little kid could be.

Then he opened his mouth and threw up all over my chest.

I cleaned up the vomit, but I still wasn't finished. I had to keep bouncing him until it was time to give him a bottle...which wasn't for another 45 minutes. The slightest pause would result in immediate crying. And I really just wanted to crawl back into bed.

But I kept on bouncing him. Mrs. Stevenson would have been so proud...

AN EVERYDAY LIE

Have you ever noticed how everything around us is pretty much the same?

Look at McDonalds and Wendy's and Burger King. Are they really so totally different? Okay, so the sandwiches have different names. But in the end, it's just a fast-food burger joint.

It's the same story in the music industry. And in technology (except Google...they are by far the best). And for running shoes. And TV shows. And everything in between.

Now, don't get me wrong. I like fast food. I watch my fair share of television. I listen to music and use my Android phone and all of that.

But haven't you noticed how alike stuff is? The color options may be different. And there might be upgrades if you want to pay for them. But at the core, it's really all the same.

"So what, Joel? I don't see the problem."

Well, it's not a problem. As long as you're only talking about hamburgers or smart phones.

But when you start to think this way about people...it becomes a big problem.

It becomes Lie #6.

Lie #6 says that everyone is basically the same. People are all the same.

This Lie says people have different noses and preferences and abilities. But at heart, they're just people. They may have philosophies and religions that sound totally different, but that's just about believing something. No matter what you believe, just believe it "with all your heart." Because people are just people...and in the end, we're all the same.

But Lie #6 has one major flaw. We aren't all the same.

It's kind of like my two babies.

They were both small. They both had big heads. They had two arms and two legs. They cried. They had to be carried around. I had to be aware of both of them at all times.

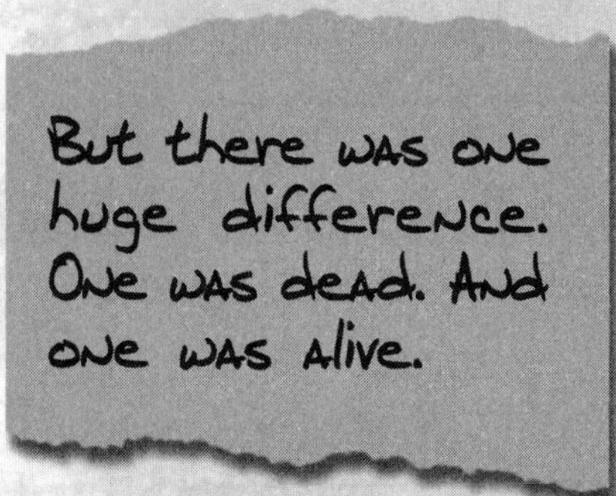

In many ways, they were exactly the same. But they weren't. They were FUNDAMENTALLY different.

And what is the big difference?

Life. The babies might have looked similar on the outside. They both had legs and arms. But there was one huge difference. One was dead. And one was alive.

One baby was a computer. The other was a living, breathing little human being. One made a crying noise because its internal timer went off. The other cried because he was hungry or lonely or covered in poop. One was a piece of teaching equipment like a history book or a graphing calculator. The other was a real baby with real emotions...and real poop.

Alike on the outside, but still FUNDAMENTALLY different in the most important way imaginable. And to think otherwise would have been a big mistake.

Just like believing Lie #6.

See, a lot of people think that Christians and Hindus and Muslims and Buddhists and atheists all have their own beliefs, so they're basically all alike. Sure, they may dress differently or have their own lists of rules to follow. But deep down, they think people are still "just people" no matter what they believe.

Maybe you think that, too.

Well, let me burst that bubble for you right now. Christians and Hindus and Muslims and Buddhists and atheists and all other people out there...are NOT the same.

No matter what it might look like, Christians are immensely different from all people. It's not just the fact that Christians have different beliefs. I'm not talking about beliefs. I'm saying Christians aren't "just people."

Christians are totally, radically, FUNDAMENTALLY different. Christians, unlike everyone else, are truly...ALIVE.

NEW LIFE

"So, are you saying that all non-Christians are dead?"

Yep. But let me explain.

Up to this point, we've covered how people can "get right" with God. It's all because of Jesus. Jesus came to rescue us. He died as our SINLESS Substitute so that we could be forgiven and reconciled to God. It's all a gift from God (grace) which we receive when we make the turn of faith from ourselves to Jesus (see Lie #5).

But that doesn't really make Christians different. It makes their circumstances different; they are forgiven. They have been reconciled to God. They have the promise of life after death. But if that's all, then Christians are just like everyone else, only with different circumstances.

But the Bible says that's not all. The Bible says that when we make that turn of faith, God doesn't just change our CIRCUMSTANCES, He changes US.

Think about it as the work of a handyman versus the work of a surgeon. A handyman fixes your house, which changes your CIRCUMSTANCES. A surgeon fixes your body, which changes YOU.

God is a handyman and a surgeon. He changes our CIRCUMSTANCES and US.

Christians are literally changed into new people. People who are FUNDAMENTALLY different from everyone else.[1]

Now, you know that I'm a Christian. So, you might think that I'm just being cocky. Or that I think I'm special. And you might be right.

But this isn't really about whether or not I'm cocky. As usual, this is about what the Bible says. Check it out:

> ...you have been born again, not of perishable seed but of imperishable, through the living and abiding word of God; for
>
> > All flesh is like grass and all its glory like the flower of grass.
> > The grass withers, and the flower falls,
> > but the word of the Lord remains forever.
>
> And this word is the good news that was preached to you. So put away all malice and all deceit and hypocrisy and envy and all slander. Like newborn infants, long for the pure spiritual milk, that by it you may grow up into salvation if indeed you have tasted that the Lord is good. (1 Peter 1:22–2:3)

In the passage, we get an overview of how different Christians really are. Let's break it down...

NEW LIFE - IT'S REAL

The Bible says that people who turn to Jesus in faith have a brand NEW Life. Check out this verse:

> **you have been born again**

At the start of our physical lives, we are **born** into this world. When we make the turn of faith to trust in Jesus, we are literally **born again** into a NEW Life. We experience a FUNDAMENTAL, deep-down, all-encompassing change.[2]

It's like baking a cake. Mmm...cake. Yummy. As a 275-pound, former college football player, I know something about cake. And one thing I know is that it illustrates my point pretty well.

Think about it.

As a 275-pound, former college football player, I know something about cake.

You start with batter. But you don't eat batter (well, maybe a few licks...). You want cake. So there has to be a change. You put the pan into the oven, and the heat changes the liquid batter into a solid cake. That's the kind of change the Bible is talking about here. When we put our faith in Jesus, He turns us into something totally new.[3]

(And on an unrelated note, if you like whipped icing on your cake, there is something wrong with you. Butter cream icing is far superior. I'm just saying...)

But the mental image of a cake (although yummy and drool-inducing) is a little misleading. It shows an external, obvious-from-the-outside type of change. But what happens to Christians is an INTERNAL change. We are **born again** INTERNALLY.[4]

"But what exactly does that mean?"

Well, thankfully, Jesus Himself explained it for us.

Jesus said, "**Unless one is born again he cannot see the kingdom of God... that which is born of the flesh is flesh, and that which is born of the Spirit is spirit.**" (John 3:4, 6)

In other words, according to Jesus, to be **born again** means that you are "**born** of the Spirit." Just like a baby's birth begins his physical life, a person **born** of the Spirit gets a NEW spiritual Life.[5]

"Um...Spirit?"

Just hang in there...Jesus is talking about God's Spirit, aka The Holy Spirit.

Now I know some people hear "Holy Spirit," and they think of some crazy, out of control "Christian Being" that only shows up at loud church services. But for now, set aside any ideas of the "Holy Spirit" that you have heard, and let's just consider what the Bible says about the Spirit.

The Holy Spirit creates this huge change that we're talking about here. A Christian is **born again**, literally transformed on the inside, when the Spirit enters his life.[6]

And this NEW Life is totally real. It's something we EXPERIENCE. We become different, and we KNOW it.[7]

The Bible describes the experience of being **born again** in many ways:

- We had a heart of stone, but we are given a heart of flesh.[8]

- We were lost, but we are found.[9]
- We were old, but we are made new.[10]
- We were dead, but we are made alive.[11]

The NEW Life is absolutely real. And it is as different from the old life as my real son is different from that electronic baby. Completely, FUNDAMENTALLY different.

"Cool...but does this NEW Life just wear off (like my deodorant)?"

The Bible answers that question next.

NEW LIFE - IT'S PERMANENT

Okay. I'm about to make you vomit. Like worse than I vomit when I watch Biggest Loser. And way worse than my baby did when I bounced him around that night. BIG. TIME. VOMIT.

I'm going to talk about the fact that your parents had sex! HA! Your worst nightmare, I know.

"Seriously, Joel? My parents having sex?"

Don't worry...this sex talk is way different than the one you might have heard when you were a kid.

I hope you will listen in and resist the temptation to throw this book out of a moving car.

I remember when my dad gave me "the talk." He waited for a time when we were both trapped in a moving car so I couldn't leave. I think we were going like 55 mph down a county road. But, believe me, I thought about jumping out. And honestly, I'm not sure if I listened much, just because I kept thinking how awkward it was. But I hope you will listen in and resist the temptation to throw this book out of a moving car.

"Come on, Joel...is this completely necessary to include in your book?"

Yes. It is. And I'll show you why...but first, read the next section of our passage from the Bible.

> **You have been born again, not of perishable seed but of imperishable, through the living and abiding word of God**
>
> **"All flesh is like grass and all its glory like the flower of grass.**
> **The grass withers, and the flower falls,**
> **but the word of the Lord remains forever."**
> **And this word is the good news that was preached to you.**

Okay, boys and girls, here comes your Bible sex talk...

You are a human being. That means you have a Daddy who planted his "**seed**" in your Mommy. (Ha! I'm actually laughing as I'm writing this.)

But, all joking aside...God calls the **seed** from your father "**perishable seed**" because it produced a real living body of **flesh** (you) that will eventually **perish** (die).

BUT...

If you are a Christian, your Heavenly Father (God) also planted His **seed**...in your soul.

God calls what He planted in you "**imperishable seed**" (aka "**God's word**") because it produced a real living spiritual child who will never **perish** (die).[12]

So our physical bodies **wither** like **grass**. But our spiritual lives last (**remain**) **forever**.[13]

Are you getting this? Maybe the sex language is too distracting or maybe it all just sounds too simple...but that is exactly how it works.

Hearing the **word of God** is what leads to our NEW Life.

"And what exactly is the word of God?"

The **word of God** is the story of the REAL God. It's the story of how Jesus came to earth, died as our SINLESS Substitute and rose from the dead (see Lies #4 and #5).[14] It's **the good news that was preached to you** (or written to you). It's often called "the gospel" which literally means "**good news**."[15]

So we know this NEW Life will never wear off because its source is the **word of God** which **remains forever**.

Now I know all this NEW Life stuff might sound hard to believe. But, trust me. It's real. I know because I experienced it when I was in high school.[16]

NEW LIFE - IT HAPPENED TO ME

I grew up as a church kid.

And I called myself a Christian because I did things that Christians did. I went to church. I sat in the pews. I sang the songs. I was even pretty good at praying out loud. So I figured I was good to go.

Every now and then I'd hear someone talk about their "relationship with Jesus" or being "born again." But I figured it was just *church talk*, just something religious people said.

I mean, I was a pretty smart kid. I knew what a personal relationship was. I knew I had that with my sisters and my

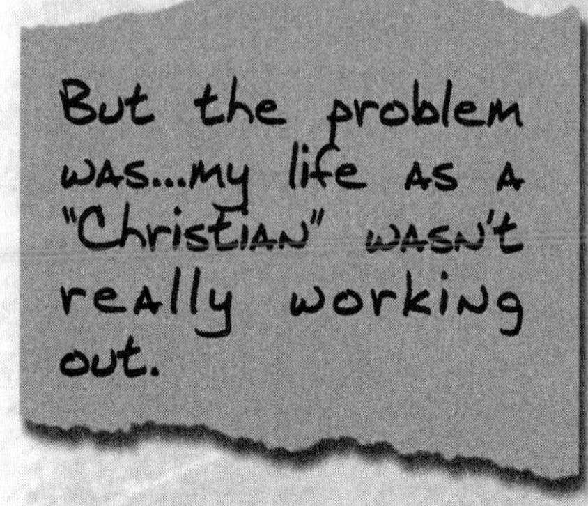

friends and my parents. But I thought Jesus was in some faraway place called heaven. So a "personal relationship" would honestly just be impossible. It just wouldn't work.

And being "born again"? I figured that was some crazy Bible metaphor that I didn't understand. No reason to take it literally.

But the problem was...my life as a "Christian" wasn't really working out.

Football was my greatest treasure. I thought that if I could play enough games or make enough tackles, I would find real happiness and significance. But my FAKE god never gave me either of those things.

Deep down, I kind of knew things weren't right. I just felt lonely, empty, unfulfilled and broken.

And sometimes, riding on that lawn mower, I even thought about it...but not too often. It made me uncomfortable to think about those things. Death, especially, scared me because I didn't really know what would happen after I died (see Lie #1).

And that's where things stayed...until my freshman year of high school.

That year, for the first time, I really heard and understood the gospel. A youth pastor explained how Jesus came to Earth, took my punishment in death, and rose from the dead. And he told me that through faith in Him, I could be forgiven and reconciled to God.

Suddenly everything made sense. I made the turn of faith to Jesus. And immediately, my life began to change. Everything was new! I developed new passions, new desires, new purpose, new hope. It was like I had been spiritually born again just like I heard people talk about. And for the first time, I knew what it meant to have a relationship with Jesus. It wasn't crazy at all.

All this stuff about "NEW Life" and "born again" is not just some religious "church talk." What the Bible is talking about here is totally real. When I heard the gospel and put my faith in Jesus, I was born again into a real, indestructible, NEW Life!

Just like the Bible said would happen.

NEW LIFE - IT GROWS

All right, so if you put your faith in Jesus after hearing the word of God, you have a brand NEW indestructible spiritual life. Cool.

But here's the thing. Being born isn't the end of your physical life. It's the beginning. And being **born again** isn't the end of a spiritual journey; it is the beginning.

So now we need to talk about how you can actually LIVE this NEW Life.

"Yeah, so how does it work? What am I supposed to do?"

Well, I'll tell you. But first, I need to make one thing very clear. Actually our passage from the Bible makes it clear:

> **You have been born again...So put away...**

Now, here's a quick English lesson. (You can thank me later.) The word **so** in a sentence means that what's coming next is BECAUSE of what came before. Look up at the verse again to see what I mean.

The passage is about to give some really practical instructions about how to live our NEW Life for God. But we don't just do these things because we think we should. And we don't do them because we think God will be impressed.

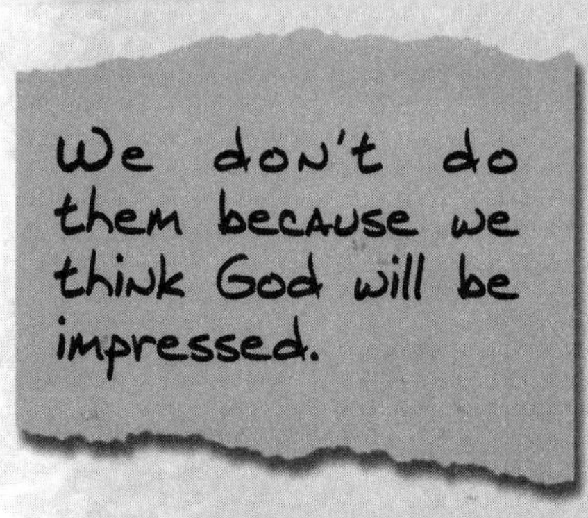

We do them, we follow the practical instructions to live our NEW Life, BECAUSE we have been born again.

Did you get that?

We are born again so we live for God.

We are forgiven so we live for God.

We are accepted so we live for God.

We are loved so we live for God.

We don't live for God in order to be born again. We live for God BECAUSE we have already been born again into a NEW Life.[17]

Got it?...Good...Let's get going.

NEW LIFE - IT'S A PROCESS

Living your NEW Life can be thought of as a 4-step process.[18]

Check it out:

> You have been born again...So put away all malice and all deceit and hypocrisy and envy and all slander. Like newborn infants, long for the pure spiritual milk, that by it you may grow up

into salvation—if indeed you have tasted that the Lord is good.

Step 1: Take Off

I have a confession to make: I wear the same shirt every time I speak. Seriously, I have a shirt that I like, and since I speak to a different audience every time, it works. It's kind of like my uniform. (Stop judging me...Jesus says that's a sin!)[19]

But here is the problem: I travel for like a week at a time. So...sometimes I wear my shirt for several days before it gets washed. (Again, stop judging me.)

Okay. So, I know I might be in the minority here because I do this with a shirt. But you gotta admit, you probably do the same thing with your jeans...don't you?

Haven't you ever been in a situation when, all of a sudden, you realize that your clothes stink? Maybe you've been in a weird-smelling restaurant or maybe you've just been wearing them all day (or all week).

But you do a quick sniff check, and you realize there is only one real option: you've got to get out of those clothes... ASAP.

"My parents having sex, now taking clothes off...what's wrong with you Joel?"

Again, I swear I have a point. And here it is.

After we put our faith in Jesus, we still have many of the sins of our "old life" wrapped around ourselves like old stinky clothes. Those evil actions of our old life are a stench to God, and we need to ditch (**put away**) them...now.[20]

"Got some examples?"

Sure. Here are the five mentioned in the passage:

1. **Malice**. Picking on the small kid in class. Slashing some stranger's tire. It's being mean...just to be mean.
2. **Deceit.** Saying you'll meet a friend for lunch when you have no intention of showing up.
3. **Hypocrisy**. Pretending to be something you absolutely aren't.
4. **Envy**. Getting upset because your friend got the scholarship you wanted. Quitting the football team because someone else got the starting spot at quarterback.
5. **Slander**. Telling lies about that neighborhood kid you don't like. Telling your friend the "latest" rumor, not caring whether or not it's true.

After we put our faith in Jesus, we still have many of the sins of our "old life" wrapped around ourselves like old stinky clothes.

So...yeah. That's all pretty nasty stuff, right? And those are just a few examples. There are all sorts of things we should stop doing now that we are Christians. Actions that don't fit with the NEW Life we've been given. They stink because they don't honor God. And we need to take them off like an old, stinky shirt BECAUSE we have been **born again**.

Step 2: Put ON

But just taking off the old stuff is not enough. Just like taking off our dirty clothes is not enough.

I cannot tell you how good it feels to put on clean clothes after a few nights of crazy travel and eating in restaurants. It's so refreshing for me and way less offensive to the people who are around me!

And just like that, we need to "put on" clean clothes, too. We need to start doing new stuff. Stuff that honors God.

"So, what kind of stuff?"

Well, right before our passage, the Bible gives us an example: "**Love one another earnestly from a pure heart, since you have been born again**" (1 Peter 1:22).

We're supposed to put on stuff like **love** for others.

And there are lots of other "clothes" that we should put on. "**Put on then...compassionate hearts, kindness, humility, meekness, and patience...**" (Colossians 3:12-14).

All these good things (along with many others found in the Bible[22]) are like new clothes we're supposed to wear. And remember, these are the qualities that should mark our NEW Life **since** (because) **we have been born again.**

Step 3: Eat

> **Like newborn infants, long for the pure spiritual milk, that by it you may grow up into salvation.**

So when my first son was born, I got schooled on all the potential problems to look out for early in our baby's life. One problem that some babies have is called "Failure to Thrive." You can probably figure out what it means, but I'll tell you just in case.

Parents bring their kid in for a checkup, and they notice that their baby hasn't gained any weight. This is a problem because babies are supposed to grow. (You can thank me later for that one, too.)

Doctors will tell you that "Failure to Thrive" is often the result a very simple problem: failure to eat. (My mother says that when I was a baby I suffered from the opposite problem: failure to stop eating...I think I still have that problem.)

Anyway, when you put your faith in Jesus, you are like a **newborn infant** in this NEW Life God has given you. And **newborns** need to eat. They need **milk**. Physical babies need physical **milk**. Spiritual babies need **spiritual milk**.

Pure spiritual milk is the **word of God**.[23]

It was the **word of God** that brought about your NEW birth, and it is the word of God that enables you to **grow up** in your NEW Life.[24]

This means that you need to consume the BIBLE (the written **word of God**).

Read it. Study it. Memorize it. Think about it. **Long for** it. ALL. THE. TIME. As you do, you will **grow up** into the person God created you to be.

And you'll realize the importance of step 4...

Step 4: Repeat

So here's the thing. After completing Step 3 (a delicious serving of Bible reading), you are going to realize you have a big problem: you weren't finished with Steps 1 and 2.

As the Spirit of God goes to work in your heart and mind as you read Scripture, you will see more evil (stinky clothing) in your life that needs to be taken off. You will also see that you lack good (clean clothing) that needs to be put on.[25]

You may even find that some of the evil you took off has snuck back on and some of the good you put on has fallen off.[26] (We are all a mess.)[27]

And that means...it's time to repeat.

Pray to God. Ask Him for forgiveness (He's always ready to give it[28]) and ask Him for help (He's always ready to give that, too[29]) as you start over.[30]

And that's the process:

- Step 1. "Take off" the dirty clothes (evil) in your life that you know won't honor God.
- Step 2. "Put on" the clean clothes (good) that you know would honor God.
- Step 3. "Eat" some spiritual food (the Bible), learning more about who God is and revealing more evil and lack of good in your life.
- Step 4. Repeat. (Praying to God for forgiveness and help.)

And that's how we grow in our NEW Life.

It's a continual process for the rest of our lives, but somehow, thanks to God's grace, we become more and more like the people God created us to be.[31] We begin to see what it looks like to worship the REAL God. And with his help, we begin to really LIVE this NEW Life.

NEW LIFE - IT KEEPS HAPPENING TO ME

Now...this all may sound kind of over the top, but it really is important.

I know because I have seen it in my own life.[32]

That initial change, that born again experience my freshman year of high school was incredible. But growing in my NEW Life since then has been even more incredible.

After becoming a Christian, I had new desires to live for God. I didn't really understand this cycle, but I just naturally tried to stop doing bad stuff, start doing good stuff, and read my Bible. As I did that, I really began to see a lot of changes in my life. I could tell that I was growing.

But, when I got to college, something changed. My desire to live for God continued, but I didn't feel like I was growing. I wasn't seeing any real changes in my life.

So I took a step back. I tried to figure out what was missing. It didn't take long to see the problem.

I hadn't been Eating (reading my Bible). I had been reading Christian books and going to church services and Bible studies, but I never really exposed myself to much more than just a handful of the more popular passages in the Bible. And as a result, I wasn't pushed back to steps 1 and 2 of the cycle (Take Off and Put On). I was starving myself spiritually.

I asked God to forgive me for neglecting His word and to help me be more committed to the Bible. I began reading and studying the Bible on my own more consistently, and the result was amazing.

I began to see huge signs of growth in my life as the Bible continually showed me the evil I needed to Take Off and the good I needed to Put On.

I was starving myself spiritually.

I've found that it's possible to skip other steps as well, but of course, it's not a good thing. A Christian who only Takes Off, but never Puts On, will never grow. And a Christian who ONLY does step #3 (Eat) might know a lot of the Bible, but will never put it into action in everyday life. That's not real growth either.[33]

All four steps are important, and I have seen that when I do them, my life changes.

This thing is real.

NEW LIFE - IT'S GENUINE

Now...there's one last thing that I need to mention here.

As you can guess, it's possible to have a "fake" NEW Life.[34] In fact, a lot of people do.[35] They say a lot of the right words, they do a lot of the right things, but inside...they were never really **born again**.[36]

So...what about you? Are you faking?

Maybe you aren't sure. In that case, the Bible actually gives a way to find out if you are genuine.

> **...that by it you may grow up into salvation if indeed you have tasted that the Lord is good.**

Do you get it?

If you put your faith in Jesus, and it's for real, **growing up** WILL happen. It's guaranteed.[37]

The Bible tells us to "**examine ourselves , to see whether you are in the faith**" (2 Corinthians 13:5).

In other words, you gotta ask yourself, "Am I really **growing**?" Because the Bible says that I WILL **grow up if indeed I've tasted that the Lord is good**.

So...let me ask you again. If you call yourself a Christian, then, are you **growing**? Is your life changing?

If you haven't seen consistent change in your life (and keep in mind that Christians still have ups and downs), then maybe you need a reality check. If you are more interested in still

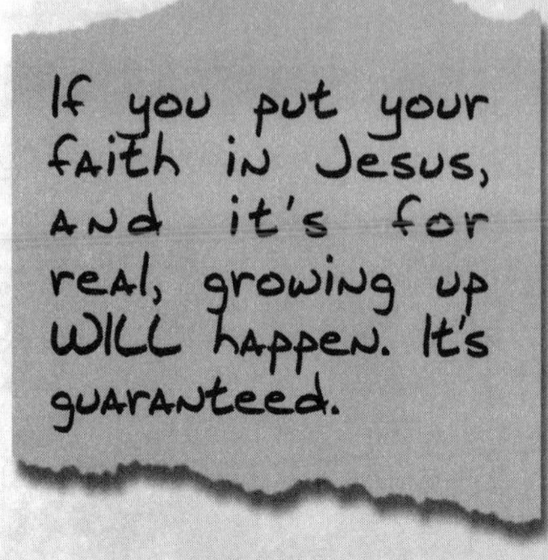

doing the same old stuff instead of living for God, then maybe you need to step back and ask whether or not you've really put your faith in Jesus.[38]

Seriously.

Because when you really connect with God, nothing's gonna keep your NEW Life from moving forward.

THE TRUTH

So there it is. Lie #6 says that all people are the same.

But it's a lie. Obviously.

Christians are transformed people. We are **born** of the Spirit of God. We are fed by the **Word of God**. And we are changing, every day, so that the life we live slowly begins to match the NEW Life we've received.

It's an unbelievably amazing existence!

But there's one last thing you need to know. See, everything in this chapter has been about you. What God is going to do in *your* life. But God isn't focused on just you (or me).

He's got a bigger agenda. You fit into it. But you aren't all of it.

Want to know what it is?

Either way...on to Lie #7...

MAKING IT PERSONAL

1. According to the Bible passage in this chapter, what makes Christians FUNDAMENTALLY different than all other people?

___

___

___

2. Do you think the idea of being "born again" is hard for people to understand? How would you explain it to someone else?

___

___

___

3. Was Joel's "Bible Sex Talk" helpful or just painful? Why do you think it is important to understand that the NEW Life is the result of "imperishable seed"?

___

___

___

4. Which step of the cycle do you think is the most challenging? "Taking off" the old way of life? "Putting on" the new way of life? Consuming the word of God? Or doing the process repeatedly? Why?

___

___

___

5. How consistent are you about "consuming" the Bible? Do you crave it, the way a baby craves milk? What would happen if you ate physical food the way you consume the word of God?

____

____

____

6. What would it look like for someone to "fake" the NEW Life? Based on the Bible passage in this chapter, how can you know if you're faking it?

____

____

____

NOTES

[1] C.S. Lewis. *Mere Christianity* (San Francisco: HarperCollins, 2001) 181.

[2] 2 Corinthians 5:17 - *Therefore, if anyone is in Christ, he is a new creation. The old has passed away; behold, the new has come.*

[3] Wayne Grudem. *Systematic Theology: An Introduction to Biblical Doctrine* (Grand Rapids: Zondervan, 1994) 701.

[4] The internal change will have external effects, but the new birth (regeneration) itself is internal.

[5] For the record, I believe that physical life starts at conception. What I (and perhaps the Bible) mean by using birth in this way is that physical birth signifies the beginning of a physical life in an obvious way.

[6] Romans 8:9 - *You, however, are not in the flesh but in the Spirit, if in fact the Spirit of God dwells in you. Anyone who does not have the Spirit of Christ does not belong to him.*

[7] Romans 8:16 - *The Spirit himself bears witness with our spirit that we are children of God,*

[8] Ezekiel 36:26 - *And I will give you a new heart, and a new spirit I will put within you. And I will remove the heart of stone from your flesh and give you a heart of flesh.*

[9] Luke 15:8–10 - *"Or what woman, having ten silver coins, if she loses one coin, does not light a lamp and sweep the house and seek diligently until she finds it? And when she has found it, she calls together her friends and neighbors, saying, 'Rejoice with me, for I have found the coin that I had lost.' Just so, I tell you, there is joy before the angels of God over one sinner who repents."*

[10] 2 Corinthians 5:17 - *Therefore, if anyone is in Christ, he is a new creation. The old has passed away; behold, the new has come.*

[11] Colossians 2:13 - *And you, who were dead in your trespasses and the uncircumcision of your flesh, God made alive together with him, having forgiven us all our trespasses,*

[12] John 10:28 - *I give them eternal life, and they will never perish, and no one will snatch them out of my hand.*

[13] 1 John 2:17 - *And the world is passing away along with its desires, but whoever does the will of God abides forever.*

[14] 1 Corinthians 15:3–4 - *For I delivered to you as of first importance what I also received: that Christ died for our sins in accordance with the Scriptures, that he was buried, that he was raised on the third day in accordance with the Scriptures,*

[15] "Gospel." Dictionary.com, 2011. Web. 21 July 2011.

[16] I am not saying that the primary reason I know the NEW Life is real is my personal experience. The primary reason I know is because the Bible says so, and I have been convinced by the Holy Spirit that the word of God is true. What I mean by "I know" in this instance is that, through experience, I have obtained a different type of knowledge.

[17] Colossians 3:12 - *Put on then, as God's chosen ones, holy and beloved, compassionate hearts, kindness, humility, meekness, and patience,*

[18] I'm not trying to be reductionistic here, just practical. That is why I said it "can be thought of" this way.

[19] Matthew 7:1 - *Judge not, that you be not judged.*

[20] Ephesians 4:22 - *to put off your old self, which belongs to your former manner of life and is corrupt through deceitful desires.* Also, Colossians 3:8 - *But now you must put them all away: anger, wrath, malice, slander, and obscene talk from your mouth.*

[21] See note #20 above. More examples can be found throughout all of Scripture.

[22] Galatians 5:22–23 - *But the fruit of the Spirit is love, joy, peace, patience, kindness, goodness, faithfulness, gentleness, self-control; against such things there is no law.*

[23] Matthew 4:4 - *But he answered, "It is written, 'Man shall not live by bread alone, but by every word that comes from the mouth of God.'"*

[24] John 17:17 - *Sanctify them in the truth; your word is truth.*

[25] Hebrews 4:12 - *For the word of God is living and active, sharper than any two-edged sword, piercing to the division of soul and of spirit, of joints and of marrow, and discerning the thoughts and intentions of the heart.* Also, 2 Timothy 3:16 - *All Scripture is breathed out by God and profitable for teaching, for reproof, for correction, and for training in righteousness,*

[26] Romans 7:18 - *For I know that nothing good dwells in me, that is, in my flesh. For I have the desire to do what is right, but not the ability to carry it out.*

[27] Romans 7:19 - *For I do not do the good I want, but the evil I do not want is what I keep on doing.* Also, Romans 7:24 - *Wretched man that I am! Who will deliver me from this body of death?*

[28] Psalm 86:5 - *For you, O Lord, are good and forgiving, abounding in steadfast love to all who call upon you.* Also, 1 John 1:9 - *If we confess our sins, he is faithful and just to forgive us our sins and to cleanse us from all unrighteousness.*

[29] Hebrews 4:16 - *Let us then with confidence draw near to the throne of grace, that we may receive mercy and find grace to help in time of need.*

[30] Bettenson, 206. This is the first line of Luther's 95 Theses.

[31] Romans 8:29 - *For those whom he foreknew he also predestined to be conformed to the image of his Son, in order that he might be the firstborn among many brothers.*

[32] See note #16

[33] James 1:22 - *But be doers of the word, and not hearers only, deceiving yourselves.*

[34] 1 John 2:4 - *Whoever says "I know him" but does not keep his commandments is a liar, and the truth is not in him,*

[35] Matthew 7:21–22 - *"Not everyone who says to me, 'Lord, Lord,' will enter the kingdom of heaven, but the one who does the will of my Father who is in heaven. On that day many will say to me, 'Lord, Lord, did we not prophesy in your name, and cast out demons in your name, and do many mighty works in your name?'*

[36] Matthew 7:23 - *And then will I declare to them, 'I never knew you; depart from me, you workers of lawlessness.'*

[37] 1 John 2:3 - *And by this we know that we have come to know him, if we keep his commandments.*

[38] James 2:18 - *But someone will say, "You have faith and I have works." Show me your faith apart from your works, and I will show you my faith by my works.*

LIE #7:

"IT'S JUST YOU AND JESUS."

A Lesson From Saving Private Ryan

I have a confession to make: I like violence.

As a little kid, I loved toy weapons. Guns, knives, swords...all fantastic entertainment. I loved playing football because it was the only time it was acceptable to hit other kids. Even after I became a Christian, violence has continued to intrigue me.

Now I believe that a healthy fascination with violence is a good and natural thing that helps me protect my family from danger. But maybe it's a bad thing that I need to "take off" (see Lie #6). Maybe I need to see a psychologist about it. I don't know. I'm still working it out. All I'm saying is that I like violence.

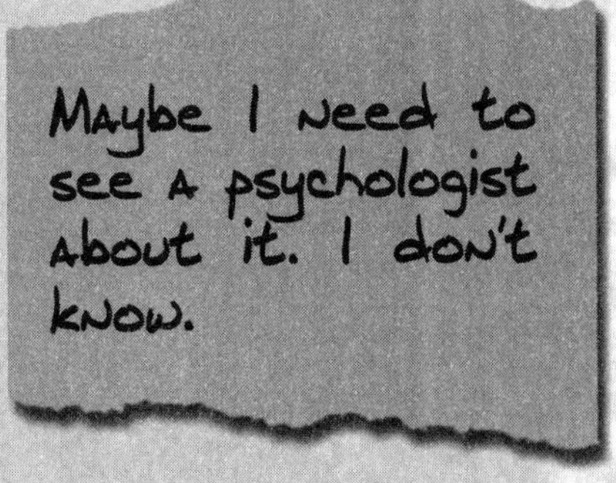

Of course, I don't play with toy guns anymore. I don't even play football anymore. But, occasionally, I watch violence on TV. Stuff like UFC and war movies.

One of my favorite war movies is *Saving Private Ryan*.

Tom Hanks plays John Miller, an Army Captain in World War II. He leads a unit of seven soldiers behind enemy lines to find a soldier named James Ryan who is the last living son of a mother who has lost three other sons in WWII.

About halfway through the movie, Captain Miller and his men stumble upon a bunker with an armed enemy machine gun. Luckily, the enemy doesn't know they are there.

With the sun blazing down on their backs, the unit huddles up to discuss the next step. As they are discussing, Captain Miller quickly begins to assemble his gear for an attack.

His men are less enthusiastic and voice their concerns.

Captain Miller is unconvinced by their objections. He tells his unit that they must take out the machine gun to protect other American troops that may come along.

Still unsure, a soldier pipes up, "It seems like an unnecessary risk, given our objective."

Without hesitation, the captain replies, "Our objective is to win the War!"

Then he leads his men in the attack.

BOOM. That's what I'm talkin' 'bout Tom Hanks!

AN EVERYDAY LIE

Wow. Seriously?

These guys are in the Army. They are supposed to be some of the greatest and most heroic men around. Not only that, they are expected to follow orders without question.

Yet, these guys, just like all of us, were determined to take the easy way out.

The soldiers in *Saving Private Ryan* give us a great picture of Lie #7.

Lie #7 says, "It's just you and Jesus." And Christians everywhere believe this. "As long as I have faith in Jesus and I'm growing (see Lies #5 and #6), then I'm good to go. My 'journey with God' is personal."

When Lie #7 creeps into our thinking, we act just like those soldiers. Captain Miller's men were looking only at their platoon's order: find Private Ryan and bring him back. But they had forgotten the big picture.

So Captain Miller reminded them. They were part of something huge: World War II.

Their team wasn't just their seven-man unit. They had a bigger team - the US Army. Their mission wasn't just to save Private Ryan. They had a bigger mission - To Win the War.

Everything else was secondary.

THE TEAM

In high school, I was a wrestler and a football player. These two sports are completely different. I'm sure you know this. But, when I think about the differences between the two sports, one in particular stands out to me.

"The Leotard...I mean...singlet? Haha. Joel wore a singlet!"

Very funny. No.

You see, people often call wrestling (and other sports like it) an "individual sport." Each guy does his own thing when it's his turn. And the result of each match is plugged into the overall team score.

Football is completely different. Each team has eleven men on the field at a time. And every player depends on every other player on every play. They function as a whole. The players' strengths and weaknesses complement one another.

If two equally talented wrestlers from different schools switched teams in the middle of a season, it wouldn't make a huge difference. The two teams would still function in the same way.

But...if two football players made the same switch in the middle of the season? Wow. That would throw just about everything off. The harmony of the teams would be totally messed up. The two players wouldn't be able to contribute to their new teams until they learned the new system and how to work with their new teammates.

Now that's what I call a "Team Sport."

So...here's the point: thinking that it's "just you and Jesus" is a fundamental misunderstanding of what it means to live the NEW Life. That makes Christianity sound like an "individual sport." It's not.

Christians aren't on a wrestling team. They are on a football team.

It's called "The Church."

THE CHURCH

Yep. That's right. It's time to talk about what some people consider to be the most boring topic in the entire world: the Church.

Now I don't think the Church is boring. And I'm pretty sure that people who do think the Church is boring have just been around too many "church people"...who are usually very boring.[1]

But boring or not, God has a lot to say about the Church. And the Bible talks about the Church like it's a TEAM.

Not a building.
Not a Sunday morning meeting.
Not a social club.
Not a charity.

No, the Church is a team of PEOPLE, God's people, who have been born again to a NEW Life. Sitting in a building that has a steeple doesn't mean that you're on the team. The turn of faith to Jesus, our SINLESS Substitute, is what really makes you a part of the PEOPLE of God.

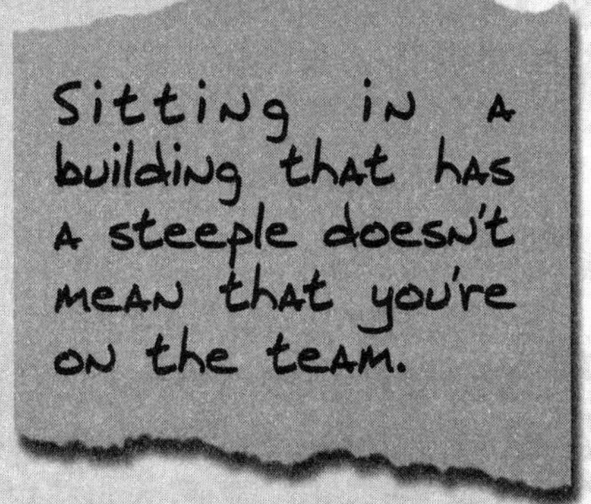

And the PEOPLE of God (the Church) are to be so organized, so focused, so unified that God says they function like a human body...Jesus' body.

Check it out:

> **For just as the body is one and has many members, and all the members of the body, though many, are one body, so it is with Christ. For in one Spirit we were all baptized into one body Jews or Greeks, slaves or free and all were made to drink of one Spirit. (1 Corinthians 12:12-13)**

Now, if you've heard anything at all about the Bible, you may have heard this passage before. But, understanding what it MEANS is incredibly important to understanding how to live your NEW Life in a way that honors God.

So let's break it down.

MANY CONNECTED PARTS

> **For just as the body is one and has many members, and all the members of the body, though many, are one body, so it is with Christ.**

A human **body** is made up of parts (**members**). Lots of them. Hands, feet, eyes, lungs, brain, heart, liver, nose. Muscles and bones and organs. The human **body** is an amazing thing. But, it's only fully functional when it's all in **one** piece.

"Well, duh, Joel."

I know, pretty simple, right? But hang with me for a minute. Because just like the human **body** only works when it's in one piece, Christ's **body** (the Church) also needs to be unified.

The day you put your faith in Jesus and were born again to a NEW Life, you were automatically made a part (**member**) of the GLOBAL Church (Jesus' **body** made up of every Christian in the world). But you also need to get CONNECTED with Jesus' **body** by becoming part of a LOCAL church. (You know...a church in your area.)

But not every Christian does that. A Christian who has bought into Lie #7 is much more...well, like a severed limb.

Think about it like this.

Did you see the Monty Python movie, *The Quest for The Holy Grail*? Well, there's a scene where King Arthur encounters the Black Knight who is guarding a bridge.

The Black Knight refuses to let him pass. When Arthur says "I must cross this bridge," the knight replies, "Then you shall die!" This, of course, leads to an epic sword fight. After only a few moments Arthur appears to secure victory when he cuts off the Black Knight's left arm. The knight, however, proclaims, "It's but a scratch!" So the fight continues.

Moments later, Arthur cuts off the Black Knight's other arm. Amazingly (and hilariously), the knight tries to continue the fight by kicking the king. Finally Arthur cuts off his right leg. And then his left.

The Black Knight, now just a bloody stump, has clearly lost the battle, but persists by yelling, "Come back here! I'll bite your legs off," as King Arthur crosses the bridge.

I know...classic.

But here's the point: the Black Knight lost four very important **members** (his arms and legs) in that fight. And those **members** proved to be completely useless when they were not connected to his **body**.

It's the same for the Church. A limb (**member**) is completely useless unless it's connected to the **body**, and a Christian who is not part of a LOCAL church is as useless as the Black Knight's severed arm. Just lying there. On the ground.

But a lot of Christians are just like that. In fact, if you're a Christian, maybe YOU are functioning that way. You aren't really part of any LOCAL church. You're a **member** disconnected from the **body**.

And what good is that?

MANY DIFFERENT PARTS

"But Joel, I'm not like church people. If I try to get connected with a local church, I won't fit in."

Eh...I don't like excuses. Remember? And that's a bad one. Look at the next part of the passage:

> **For in one Spirit we were all baptized into one body—Jews or Greeks, slaves or free—and all were made to drink of one Spirit.**

So the PEOPLE of God are all a part of **one body**. The **body** of Christ. The Church. But there are millions of us. And we are all completely different. Even in a local community, Christians have huge differences.

This is not a new problem.

When the Bible was written, there were all sorts of groups and "statuses" among Christians just like today. The examples we are given in the Bible are "**Jews or Greeks, slaves or free**."

Today you could say "the cool people and the nerds, the celebrities and the homeless." The point is this: we are all different.

But the Bible says we really can be unified because of something we have in common that is bigger than our differences. That something that we have in common is the most important quality in all the world - we have all been born again. We were all given NEW Life when The Holy Spirit entered our lives (**all were made to drink of one Spirit.**)

When we realize that we have the Holy Spirit in common, all our differences seem minor.

So, yeah. You might look and dress differently than other Christians in your area. You probably have different talents, interests and hobbies, too. It doesn't matter. All Christians are equally valuable in God's eyes. And we all need to be connected to the **Body**.

It's not "just you and Jesus"...you are part of the **Body**.

TEAM PICTURES

Of course, there are other pictures that God uses to describe his team, the PEOPLE of God. And each picture tells us something specific that helps us understand what it means to be a part of the church...

Here are a few of them:

The Family
I am the youngest of four children in my family. I have three older sisters.

When I was a kid, my dad would often take us out for ice cream after dinner. One night as we were piling in the van for an ice cream run, I decided to be a good brother by opening the van door for my sisters and then closing it once they were inside. My sister, Mollie, was the last to get in, and I firmly pulled the door shut.

Mollie screamed. I looked down and saw two of her fingertips sticking out between the door and the frame. I had shut her hand completely in the door, and it had latched shut.

I froze. I didn't know what to do. My dad ran around the van and opened the door. He and my other two sisters rushed Mollie inside so my mom could inspect the injury. She was crying a lot.

A few minutes later, my dad came back out to the garage. I was still standing beside the van. And I guess I had a very concerned look on my face because he asked me if I was going to be okay.

I answered, "So...we're still gonna go get ice cream, right?"

Horrible, I know.

And with stories like that (and we all have them), it's kind of surprising that God says that the church is a family. But He does. The Bible refers to God as our Father almost 100 times. Christians are called God's children, and we are told to consider each other our brothers and sisters in Christ.[2]

Now, ideally, families are made up of loving and intimate relationships. Families should be all about people supporting each other, being connected to each other, and showing love to each other. (Kind of like I should have done with Mollie. After I slammed her hand in the door.)

But maybe your family isn't ideal.

Maybe yours is "complicated." Maybe you've had three different men you were supposed to call "dad" just this past year. Maybe "communication" with your brother means him telling you that you will never be as good as him. Maybe you dread family gatherings because of all the drama and yelling. Maybe you have never heard your parents say, "I love you."

There are lots of families like that. Actually, there are lots of local churches like that. Some churches are more dysfunctional than the worst families I know.

Some churches are more dysfunctional than the worst families I know.

So maybe God shouldn't have picked this particular picture. Surely there were better ones, right?

No. And here's why.

Families are connected in a special way. Your friends may come and go, but your family will always be your family.

- Even if you haven't seen your brother in years, he's still family.
- Even if your dad seems to care more about work than you, he's still family.
- Even if your sister won't speak to you, she's still family.

There is a special connection that only families have.

It's the same thing with the PEOPLE of God. Christians have a special connection. We were all born again into the same spiritual family.

Sometimes family life is great, sometimes it's rough. But either way, those people are still family, so don't give up on them.[3]

It's not "just you and Jesus"...you are part of the Family.

The Flock

Another image the Bible uses to describe the Church is a flock of sheep.

Yes, sheep. Little fluffy balls of wool. They say "baa." You can order lamb chops in a restaurant (yum). You know, sheep.

And let me tell you...this isn't a flattering comparison. Sheep are really, really dumb.

See, some animals are really smart. Like horses. They can come and go on their own. They can find food and water. They can survive almost anything with very little help.

Not sheep. Sheep cannot find their way on their own. Well, sometimes they can, but if they aren't watched, they might just wander over the edge of a cliff. Seriously. I am not making this up. It happened in Turkey a couple of years ago. Over four hundred sheep just walked right off a cliff.[4]

So yeah, God compares us to one of the dumbest animals in the barnyard.

"Okay, Joel. Now you are telling me that I'm dumb?"

Well, actually, no. (Are you shocked?) At least, not THAT dumb. Jesus picked this animal to describe us for a reason that's a little different. Sheep NEED to be led. Sheep NEED a shepherd. They CANNOT survive without a leader. Literally. Look at what happened in Turkey!

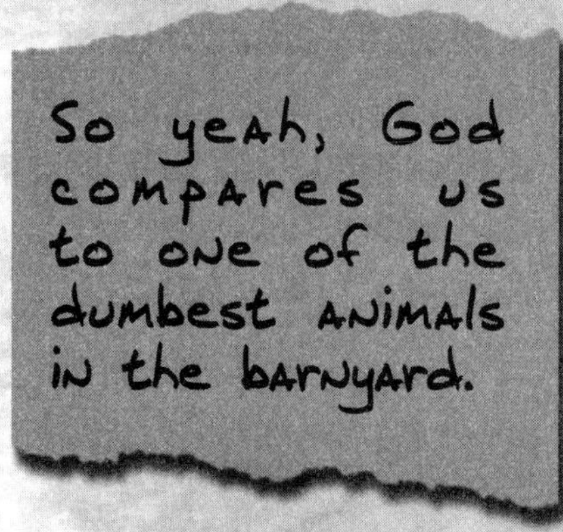

And that's why Jesus called Himself "The Good Shepherd."[5] He leads His flock (the global Church).

And amazingly, He gave local church leaders that same job, too.

Church leaders are called "elders" (many churches call them pastors), and they have been given the responsibility of teaching, leading, and shepherding God's people.[6]

Read this verse: "**So I exhort the elders among you...shepherd the flock of God that is among you, exercising oversight.**" (1 Peter 5:1-2)

"So what's your point, Joel? Elders are to be like shepherds? I'm not a pastor, so it sounds like it doesn't apply to me. Looks like I'm good!"

Actually, no. My point is a little more personal than that. If elders are shepherds, and the Church is like a flock of sheep, then what is the job of the sheep?

To FOLLOW.

Christians MUST obey the authority of their local church elders.

Now I know you probably don't like this. You probably started to twitch when you read the word "authority."

If you're like the average person, then you are probably thinking, *"I can do whatever I want...I don't have to follow anyone...I'm my own authority."*

Oh yeah, like you are so special. Sorry...you're NOT.

Just read this verse: "**Obey your leaders and submit to them, for they are keeping watch over your souls...**" **(Hebrews 13:17)**

The Bible is very clear that Christians need to follow their leaders.

And believe it or not, God had some really good reasons for establishing authority in the Church. Here are a couple:

1. Organization - When you're dealing with lots of people, someone needs to call the shots. Someone needs to make the ultimate and final decision, or nothing will get done. Authority helps us be organized and efficient.[7]

2. Protection - I know you've probably heard the saying "With great power comes great responsibility." Yeah, it's kind of cliche. But...it's also kind of true. Certain people are given authority, and they have the responsibility of looking out for others. Think about how good parents protect their children. By teaching and leading, local church elders protect Christians from spiritual dangers like evil behavior and false teaching.[8]

Now, I know some questions always come up with this topic.

Question: *"But what if my elders are complete jerks and totally evil?"*
Answer: Don't worry. There are very strict qualifications for elders in the Bible that must be met. Only the most capable and mature Christians qualify for the position. If an elder really turns out to be an evil jerk, he disqualifies himself.[9]

Question: *"But what if my elders tell me to do something that contradicts the Bible? Do I still have to obey?"*
Answer: No way. While elders have real authority, the Bible is the higher authority. So if your elders ask you to do something contrary to the Bible, you should not obey. For example: If your pastor tells you to get involved in a small group Bible study...then obey. If your pastor tells you to kill your next door neighbor...then don't obey.

Just remember, God has given us elders to protect, teach and lead us because he loves us and wants the best for us. We need to face the fact that we are sheep, and we need to follow our shepherds.

It's not "just you and Jesus"...you are part of the Flock.

The Army

The Bible also describes Christians as members of a military force:

- "Epaphroditus my brother and fellow worker and fellow soldier" (Phil. 2:25)
- "Share in suffering as a good soldier of Christ Jesus" (2 Timothy 2:3)
- "Take up the whole armor of God" (Ephesians 6:13)

For a long time, this was one of the most common pictures that the Church used to describe itself. These days, it makes people nervous to call the Church an army. Some local churches have even removed all the old songs that contain this picture.

Why? Because the picture of the military isn't very gentle. People don't want to join an army...they want to be hugged. They don't want to see Jesus as a commander-in-chief...they want a loving friend.

Don't get me wrong...Jesus is love. Jesus is a friend. And hugs are cool...I guess.

But don't think for a second that He isn't our Commander-in-Chief, too.

Remember, the Church isn't really about you. Or me. It's about Jesus. And Jesus is sending His people on a real mission in the world. Which means that...feeling loved is not our primary objective. As Captain Miller in *Saving Private Ryan* put it, "our objective is to win the war."

Of course, it would help us to know what *our* objective is. Believe it or not, God's army isn't supposed to kill people or beat them into submission to (or with) the Bible. No, Jesus wants to continue healing our broken world. And He wants to do it through us.

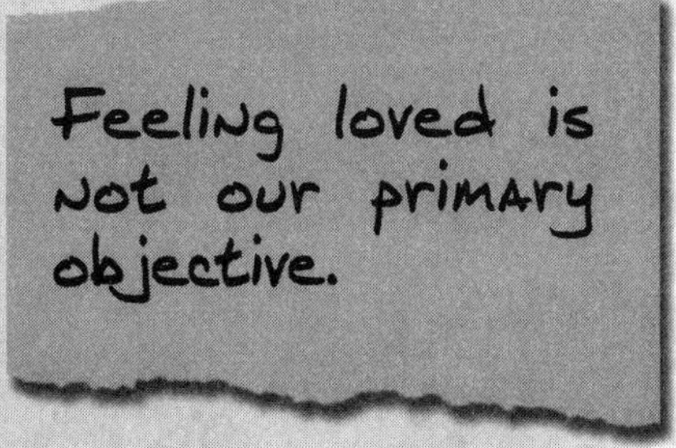

The Church's mission (objective) is to love people, to serve people, and most of all, to tell people about Jesus and teach them how to follow him.[10]

Jesus wants his Church to grow.[11] And he wants to use us to take the good news about Jesus out into the world so that more and more people will be born again into a NEW Life.

We need to be as passionate and driven about accomplishing our mission to reach the world as soldiers in the heat of battle are to complete their mission.

The fact is, we have a job to do. A job that Jesus Himself has ordered us to accomplish. And we, as His Church, have to stay "on mission" until it's complete.[12]

It's not "just you and Jesus"...you are a part of God's Army.

THE TRUTH

Lie #7 wants us to make our NEW Life about ourselves, how we feel, what we want to get out of it, where it can help us out.

The truth is...Jesus is doing something much bigger than any of that or any of us. Christians are part of the PEOPLE of God and...

- We should be unified like a human **body**...Don't be a severed limb.
- We should be loving like a close-knit family...Don't be a runaway child.
- We should be led by good shepherds...Don't be a stray sheep.
- We should be on mission like a fierce army...Don't be a soldier gone AWOL.

You have the chance to be part of what the REAL God is doing.

Take it.

It's not "just you and Jesus"...you are part of the Church.

MAKING IT PERSONAL

1. Why do you think so many Christians act like Christianity is an "individual sport"?

______

______

______

2. What excuses have you heard (or given) for not getting connected to a local church? How would you use the information in this chapter to demolish those excuses? Specifically, which Bible passages would you use?

______

______

______

3. In what ways are the PEOPLE of God like a family?

______

______

______

4. What do you think keeps people from following the leaders in a local church? Is following a church leader harmful or helpful? Why?

______

______

______

5. **Do you like the image of the Church as an army? Why or why not?**

____

____

____

6. **What mission did Jesus give his army, the PEOPLE of God, to accomplish?**

____

____

____

NOTES

1 By "church people," I mean people who attend church, but who may or may not be Christians.

2 James 2:15 - *If a brother or sister is poorly clothed and lacking in daily food,*

3 Augustine definitely understood the tension of calling the Church a family when he said, "The church is a whore, but she's my mother." (I couldn't find any written proof that Augustine said this, but it's usually credited to him.)

4 "450 Sheep Jump to their Deaths in Turkey." *USA Today*. 8 July 2005. Web. 19 July 2011.

5 John 10:11 - *I am the good shepherd. The good shepherd lays down his life for the sheep.*

6 The Bible uses the titles "elder" and "overseer/bishop" interchangeably (compare Acts 20:17-28 and Titus 1:5-7).

7 1 Timothy 5:17 - *Let the elders who rule well be considered worthy of double honor, especially those who labor in preaching and teaching.*

8 Acts 20:28 - *Pay careful attention to yourselves and to all the flock, in which the Holy Spirit has made you overseers, to care for the church of God, which he obtained with his own blood.*

9 1 Timothy 3:1–7 - *The saying is trustworthy: If anyone aspires to the office of overseer, he desires a noble task. Therefore an overseer must be above reproach, the husband of one wife, sober-minded, self-controlled, respectable, hospitable, able to teach, not a drunkard, not violent but gentle, not quarrelsome, not a lover of money. He must manage his own household well, with all dignity keeping his children submissive, for if someone does not know how to manage his own household, how will he care for God's church? He must not be a recent convert, or he may become puffed up with conceit and fall into the condemnation of the devil. Moreover, he must be well thought of by outsiders, so that he may not fall into disgrace, into a snare of the devil.*

10 Matthew 28:18–20 - *And Jesus came and said to them, "All authority in heaven and on earth has been given to me. Go therefore and make disciples of all nations, baptizing them in the name of the Father and of the Son and of the Holy Spirit, teaching them to observe all that I have commanded you. And behold, I am with you always, to the end of the age."*

[11] Matthew 16:18 - *And I tell you, you are Peter, and on this rock I will build my church, and the gates of hell shall not prevail against it.*

[12] Colossians 4:5–6 - *Walk in wisdom toward outsiders, making the best use of the time. Let your speech always be gracious, seasoned with salt, so that you may know how you ought to answer each person.* Also, 2 Corinthians 5:20 - *Therefore, we are ambassadors for Christ, God making his appeal through us. We implore you on behalf of Christ, be reconciled to God.*

THE TRUTH IS DANGEROUS

So...there you go.

Just what I promised. The facts. The truth. The stuff no one else is telling you. Or almost no one, anyway.

Here's a recap.

1. The BIG Stuff ~~can~~ can't wait.
   We use a lot of excuses to keep from facing the realities of Life, Death, and God. But the fact is...we can't avoid these questions. They're out there. They're important. And you have to start dealing with them. Today. No more excuses.

2. Google ~~has~~ doesn't have all the answers.
   Our typical sources (the internet, other people, ourselves) just won't work for questions about Life, Death, and God because they're INSIDE sources. We need an OUTSIDE Source. And the Bible is the best option we have. You can't ignore what the Bible says just because you don't like it. You need to deal with what the Bible says about the questions that we need answered.

3. It's not all good.
   No matter what you want to think...the world is not all good. WE are not all good. We screwed up by betraying the REAL God. We turned away from Him to honor and

worship every FAKE god we could invent: achievements, celebrity, friends, image, experiences, and (most of all) self. Every single one of us has betrayed God this way. Even you. We need to turn back to the REAL God.

4. God is an un-stuffed teddy bear.
   So you think you can just make God what you want Him to be? WRONG. That's how most people act, but it just isn't true. The Bible says the only REAL God is Jesus Christ. He's God on a mission, the God-man who came to die on a cross and rise from the dead. Now He's back on His throne in heaven. Don't want to think of Jesus as God? Too bad. He's it.

5. You're a winner.
   Everyone's a winner, we're told. But we're not. We suck. We betrayed God, and we cannot get back to Him on our own. Our attempts to reach God are worthless. We are guilty and deserve judgement. So God provided a solution. Jesus came to die on the cross as our SINLESS Substitute. His blood justifies us. His death reconciles us to God and saves us. And it is all a gift from God that we can receive only through faith.

6. All people are the same.
   It's all the same, right? All religions? All religious people? Just believe something. Sincerely believe it, and you'll be fine. Right? WRONG. Christians are not the same. We are totally different. We are transformed. By the power of the Holy Spirit, we are given NEW Life. And by that same power, we are able to grow and live out that NEW Life every day.

7. It's not just you and Jesus.
   Being a Christian is not just about you and Jesus. Becoming a Christian is. But after that...you are part of something much, much bigger than you could ever imagine. You are part of the PEOPLE of God, the Church. God gives us lots of pictures of what that looks like: a body, a family, a flock, an army. The reality is that it's not "just you and Jesus." You are part of the Church.

But that's it. The lies I used to believe. The lies that some of you used to believe. The lies that you may still believe.

It doesn't matter if you have been a Christian since you were six years old. It doesn't matter if you just decided to believe the truth ten minutes ago. And it doesn't matter if you still think I'm some crackpot "motivational speaker" and all this stuff is totally bogus.

Even if you don't like it, even if it's not what you wanted to hear... it's not just what I think.

This is what the Bible says. This is the truth. This is the BIG Stuff.

And now it's in your hands.

See, truth is dangerous. Once you've been handed the truth, you are now responsible for it. Once you are faced with reality as it is, not just as you want it to be, well...now you have to do something with it.

And you have two options:
1. Refuse the truth and keep feeding yourselves the lies all around you.

2. Accept the truth and turn to Jesus, the REAL God who died for you.

I've handed you the truth. You have to make your choice. Now it's up to you...

So what are you going to do?

MAKING IT PERSONAL

1. **Which Lies, if any, do you think that you were buying into?**

   ____

   ____

   ____

2. **Do you agree that the truth is "dangerous"? Why or why not?**

   ____

   ____

   ____

3. **Joel gave two main things someone could do with the truth. What reasons might someone give for taking Option #1 (refusing the truth)? Are they good reasons?**

   ____

   ____

   ____

4. **Which option are you going to take? Why?**

   ____

   ____

   ____

NOW WHAT?

Wow! You made it all the way to the end. So, that's it, right?

Well, not really.

Now that you've finished the book, you may be wondering, "Okay...now what?" Maybe you're still processing what you've read. Maybe you're ready to just toss these pages into the nearest trashcan. Maybe you're somewhere in between.

But wherever you are, I can guarantee this: there is something more you need to do.

Getting you to finish this book was never really the point. Don't get me wrong - I'm really glad you did read the whole thing. But if you just read it and walk away, then I've failed. Because I don't just want you to read.

I want you to move forward. I want you to take the next step.

And what is the next step?

Well, that kind of depends on where you are right now. So, assuming you don't think I'm completely insane, I'd guess that you can probably see yourself as one of three people.

Person 1 is thinking...*"I'm just not sure."*
Person 2 is thinking...*"I think I'm ready to turn to Jesus."*
Person 3 is thinking...*"I have put my trust in Jesus. Now how do I grow?"*

Each Person has something more he or she needs to do now. But what? Well, I have some specific encouragement for each of these people. Check it out below.

"I'M JUST NOT SURE"

Maybe you read everything I've said, but you're not really convinced yet. That's okay. But to you, I want to say three simple things.

Check your motives.
Ask yourself why you aren't sure. Is it because you don't want to let go of something? Or give up control? Did you have a bad experience with Christians? Do you still have some legitimate questions? Think through your motives and consider whether they really are good reasons to delay turning to Jesus. If you still have honest questions you need to work through, that's cool. Just don't wait around for bad reasons.

Keep wrestling.
If you are honestly wrestling through these issues, please don't stop. Keep in mind how important this stuff is. If you need time, take time, but use it wisely. Think it through, talk it through, read stuff. (*The Reason For God* by Tim Keller and *Mere Christianity* by C.S. Lewis are two great places to start.)

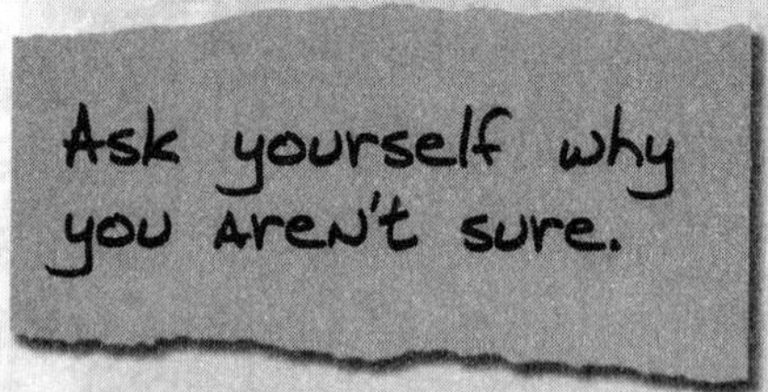

Pull the trigger.
When you come to the conclusion that Jesus is worth a step of faith, then it's time to take that step. Don't feel like you have to have all the answers. Even if you have some doubts or fears, don't worry, that's totally okay. Jesus will take you as you are. The important thing is that, if you're ready, you dive in all the way.

"I THINK I'M READY TO TURN TO JESUS."

Maybe you're ready to turn to Jesus right now. That's awesome. Here's what you need to know:

Examine your heart.
Do you *really* want to turn to Jesus? That might seem crazy for me to ask. But this is a serious deal.

Are you really willing to turn away from yourself?
Are you really willing to worship Jesus?

Don't make this decision flippantly. If you don't approach the issue seriously, then you may fool yourself into thinking you've turned to Jesus when you really haven't. It happens all the time. Don't let it happen to you.

Make the turn of faith.
Turn away from self and turn to Jesus. Put your trust in Jesus. Trust him to save you. Trust him to forgive you. Ask him for the power to truly leave your old life behind. Trust him to give you NEW Life through the power of the Holy Spirit. You may find it helpful to look back at the prayer on page 130 as an example of what the turn of faith "looks" like. But don't wait any longer. Make the turn.

Get ready to grow.
Recognize that trusting Jesus is not the end of a journey. It is the beginning of a NEW Life. A new relationship with the God of the Universe. If you've made the turn of faith, it's now time to grow.

"I HAVE PUT MY TRUST IN JESUS. NOW HOW DO I GROW?"

You might have turned to Jesus years ago or just minutes ago, but now you realize there is much more to do. No problem. Here's what you need to do next:

Read your Bible.

The best way to grow in a relationship with anyone is communication. I have a smokin' hot wife, but if we never communicate, it won't be a good relationship. It is the same with God.

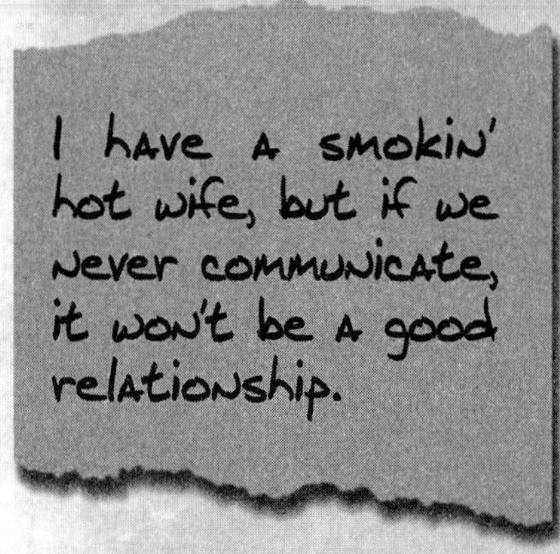

Communication with God starts with reading your Bible. Yes, there are a ton of other Christian books and resources out there which are great. But nothing should ever take the place of God's word in your life.

Why? Because reading the Bible is how we LISTEN to God. He wrote it for us. It's the best way to know more about Jesus and what He has to say to you. Get a good translation (I recommend the ESV, English Standard Version) and then set aside time EVERY DAY to read.

As you read, keep in mind the following questions:

- What does it say?
- What does it mean?
- How does it apply to my life?

And keep the cycle from Lie #6 in mind as you consider the last question. Think, "What are some of the dirty clothes I need to take off? What are some of the clean clothes I need to put on?" The goal is not just to examine the Bible, but to allow the Bible to examine you and your life, so that you can respond and grow.

Pray.
The Bible is how we listen to God. And the way we TALK to God is prayer.

Of course, He already knows our thoughts, but it's important to take the time to consciously share with God all that is in your heart and mind.

- Pray about what you have read in the Bible. Ask God to help you understand.
- Tell God how awesome He is as you learn more about Him.
- Thank Jesus for all the good He has given you and continues to give you.
- Continually ask for his forgiveness as you become aware of evil in your life.
- Pray about the things going on in your life. Ask for help.
- Pray for others.

Come to God as you would approach a good father - on a personal level, but with respect. Remember - you have been born again into God's family, so you can (and should) speak to your new Father often. Set aside some time EVERY DAY to pray.

And don't worry if it's hard to do at first. Prayer takes practice. Maybe your mind wanders or you aren't sure what to say. Try writing your prayers out or making a list of things you want to talk to God about. And try praying out loud. It may feel weird at first, but it can help keep your mind from wandering.

No matter how you do it...you need to pray. No excuses.

Connect with a local church.
Finally, you've got to get plugged in to a local church. And I mean really plugged in. Not just sitting there on Sunday mornings. Get to know the people. Let them get to know you.

Really listen to the leaders. Follow their lead. Become a real member of the body, family, flock, army.

Maybe you need to start by finding a church.

The most important thing about finding a good church is finding one that believes and teaches the Bible as the ultimate source of truth. It will be tempting to look for one that just has good music or people you like. Those things are great, but they are not nearly as important as getting the Bible right. Actually, if a church doesn't believe and teach the Bible clearly, it doesn't matter how cool or fun it is, you need to stay away from it.

So, here are a few important questions to ask when considering any particular church.

1. *Are they explaining or just telling?* - Some churches have leaders who just teach concepts and then refer to some Bible verses to support their ideas. That's not cool. It is important to find a church where the leaders SHOW what the Bible says, not just tell you what it says. You can kind of use this book as an example. I took several sections of the Bible throughout and explained what they were saying. Hopefully when I was done, you were able to see more clearly what was already there in the text. Never believe what you are being taught about the Bible until you really see it for yourself in the text. And if the leaders aren't SHOWING you what the Bible says, then it's time to move on.

2. *Is the gospel explained clearly and consistently?* - The message about Jesus dying for us and rising from the dead is at the very center of what Christianity is all about. The Bible actually says it is the most important piece of information in the world.[1] Churches should always be talking about who Jesus is and what he did for us on the cross.

If a church doesn't seem to be obsessed with the gospel, keep looking.

3. *Is there a way to really connect?* - If a church still looks good after asking the first two questions, then you should try to get connected. But remember, just attending a church isn't really connecting to it. You need to form real relationships with the leaders and people of a church so you can really be a part of what God is doing. This will take some effort on your part. Ask around if there is a way to really plug in. Some churches have small groups; others have a way to be mentored by a leader one-on-one. There might be a process for becoming a member or ways to serve. Whatever form it takes, your connection to your church needs to be REAL.

I'M DONE

All right, I'm done...and this time, I'm really finished. This is as far as I can take you.

Now it's your turn. It's up to you to take the next step.

MAKING IT PERSONAL

1. **Joel described three things someone might be thinking after reading the book. Which category do you fall into?**

___

___

___

2. **Based on Joel's advice in this final section of the book, what are YOU going to do now? Write out some of your next steps below.**

___

___

___

___

___

___

___

___

___

___

NOTES

1 1 Corinthians 15:3–4 - *For I delivered to you as of first importance what I also received: that Christ died for our sins in accordance with the Scriptures, that he was buried, that he was raised on the third day in accordance with the Scriptures,*

THANK YOUS

First, I thank Jesus who loved me and gave himself for me. I pray this book will bring glory to You, my Rescuer, my Friend, my King!

Second, I thank all of God's people who have invested themselves in my spiritual journey. This book and any impact it makes is fruit of your investment. I must thank several by name:

From the bottom of my heart (and in chronological order), I say THANK YOU...

To my Mom and Dad, for helping me understand how God loves me.

To Marcia Wise, for planting the word of God in me.

To JC Collins, for reaping my soul in the harvest of the Lord.

To CS Lewis, for helping me think hard about God.

To Jim Dunaway, for showing me how to love people.

To Ryan Holliday, for laboring beside me in the gospel.

To Bryan Hawkins, for showing me what it means to be all in for Jesus.

To Tom Rode, for teaching me to preach the gospel with strength.

To Jim Schmidtke, for teaching me to preach the gospel with boldness.

To my Bethany, for trusting me. Your trust makes this weak man strong.

To Greg Koukl, for showing me how to read the Bible.

To Mark Driscoll, for challenging me to put the Bible above my mind.

To DA Carson, for helping me make sense of the Bible as a whole.

To John Piper, for challenging me to make Jesus my greatest treasure.

To Mark Trotter, for showing me how to forget yourself in serving God.

To Joel III and Judah, for teaching me what it means to be a child of God.

To Rudy and Patricia Niswanger, for helping make this project possible.

To Shannah Hogue, for helping me turn my thoughts into this book.

I thank my God for you all!

SOURCES

"450 Sheep Jump to their Deaths in Turkey." *USA Today*. 8 July 2005. Web. 19 July 2011.

Althaus, Paul. *Theology of Martin Luther.* Google eBooks. Philadelphia: Fortress, 1966. Web. 20 July 2011.

Batman Begins. Dir. Christopher Nolan. Perf. Christian Bale. Warner Bros., 2005.

Beckwith, Francis J., and Gregory Koukl. *Relativism: Feet Firmly Planted in Mid-Air.* Grand Rapids: Baker, 1998.

Bettenson, Henry, and Chris Maunder, eds. *Documents of the Christian Church.* New ed. Oxford: Oxford, 1999.

Craig, William Lane. *Reasonable Faith: Christian Truth and Apologetics.* Wheaton, IL: Crossway, 1994.

Churchill, Winston. "MIT Mid-Century Convocation." 31 March 1949. MIT, 1999. Web. 20 July 2011.

"The Diary of a Young Girl." Wikipedia, The Free Encyclopedia, 7 Jul. 2011. Web. 20 Jul. 2011.

"Excruciate." *Online Etymological Dictionary.* 2010. Web. 20 July 2011.

Frahm, Eckart. “Assyria.” *World Book Advanced.* World Book, 2011. Web. 20 July 2011.

Geisler, Norman. *Baker Encyclopedia of Christian Apologetics.* Grand Rapids: Baker, 1999.

“Gospel.” Dictionary.com. 2011. Web. 21 July 2011.

Grudem, Wayne. *Systematic Theology: An Introduction to Biblical Doctrine.* Grand Rapids: Zondervan, 1994.

Hagelia, Hallvard. “THE FIRST DISSERTATION ON THE TEL DAN INSCRIPTION.” *SJOT: Scandinavian Journal of the Old Testament* 18.1 (2004): 135-146. Academic Search Complete. EBSCO. Web. 20 July 2011.

“Harry Potter in translation.” Wikipedia, The Free Encyclopedia, 20 July 2011. Web. 20 July 2011.

“History of Religion.” Maps-of-War. 9 Sept. 2006. Web. 20 July 2011.

The Holy Bible. English Standard Version (ESV). Crossway, 2001. Web. July 2011.

Keller, Timothy. *Counterfeit Gods: The Empty Promises of Money, Sex, and Power, and the Only Hope that Matters.* Google eBook. New York: Dutton, 2009. Web. 20 July 2011.

--. *The Reason for God: Belief in an Age of Skepticism.* New York: Riverhead, 2008.

Kercheville, Brent. “Mark 15:21-41, The Crucifixion of Jesus.” West Palm Beach Church of Christ, 2011. Web. 20 July 2011.

Lewis, C.S. *Mere Christianity.* San Francisco: HarperCollins, 2001.

Longman, Timothy. "Rwanda." *World Book Advanced.* World Book, 2011. Web.20 July 2011.

McDowell, Josh. *The Best of Josh McDowell: A Ready Defense.* Comp. Bill Wilson. Nashville: T. Nelson, 1993.

--. *The New Evidence That Demands a Verdict.* Rev. ed. Nashville: T. Nelson, 1999.

Mendilow, Jonathan. "Jerusalem." *World Book Advanced.* World Book, 2011. Web.20 July 2011.

Meyers, Carol L. "Psalms, Book of." *World Book Advanced.* World Book, 2011. Web.20 July 2011.

Monty Python and the Holy Grail. Dir. Terry Gilliam. Python (Monty) Pictures, 1974.

Moreland, J.P. *Scaling the Secular City: A Defense of Christianity.* Grand Rapids: Baker, 1987.

Packer, J.I. *Knowing God.* Downers Grove, IL: IVP, 1973.

Pascal, Blaise. *Pascal's Pensees.* New York: Dutton, 1958.

Piper, John. *The First Dark Exchange: Idolatry.* 4 Oct. 1998. DesiringGod, 2011. Web.20 July 2011.

Richardson, Seth F. C. "Babylon." *World Book Advanced.* World Book, 2011. Web.20 July 2011.

Roisman, Joseph. "Alexander the Great." *World Book Advanced.* World Book, 2011. Web.20 July 2011.

Saving Private Ryan. Dir. Steven Spielberg. Perf. Tom Hanks. Dreamworks, 1998.

Strobel, Lee. *The Case for Christ: A Journalist's Personal Investigation of the Evidence for Jesus*. Grand Rapids, MI: Zondervan, 1998.

"Tel Dan Stele." Wikipedia, The Free Encyclopedia, 1 July 2011. Web. 20 July 2011.

Walvoord, J. F., Zuck, R. B., & Dallas Theological Seminary. *The Bible Knowledge Commentary: An Exposition of the Scriptures*. Vol 2. Wheaton, IL: Victor Books, 1983.

"William Hung." Online Posting. YouTube, 7 Feb. 2008. Web. 21 July 2011. http://www.youtube.com/watch?v=9RrLQUN8UJg